DAVID KING

# Moving on from mental hospitals to community care

## A CASE STUDY OF CHANGE IN EXETER

DAVID KING

# Moving on from mental hospitals to community care

## A CASE STUDY OF CHANGE IN EXETER

The Nuffield Provincial
Hospitals Trust

Published by the
Nuffield Provincial Hospitals Trust
3 Prince Albert Road, London NW1 7SP
ISBN 0 900574 77 1

Designed by Bernard Crossland
PRINTED IN GREAT BRITAIN BY
BURGESS & SON (ABINGDON) LTD
THAMES VIEW, ABINGDON
OXFORDSHIRE

Cover illustration by New Zealand
artist Mary Taylor

# FOREWORD

After the end of World War II, reformers of social and health policy in Britain, and in some other countries, became convinced that the confinement of mentally ill people in large institutions is both dehumanising and anti-therapeutic. At one level it robs the people kept there of freedom, privacy, and normal social contact; it also denies them responsibility and control of crucial aspects of their lives. At a time when people were increasingly demanding 'rights' rather than benevolence, there was obvious cause to challenge such a system. But there was another, equally valid, reason for demanding change, when successive studies in the 50s and 60s showed that prolonged and inappropriate hospitalisation was positively inimical to modern methods of psychiatric treatment.

Yet despite the inclusion of community care in the 1959 Mental Health Act as the most appropriate form of care for mentally ill people, action to provide it was desperately slow. Nearly thirty years passed before the government was publicly committed to the idea of a comprehensive, integrated, community care system, accessible to people with mental health problems wherever they happen to live. Without farsighted managers and practitioners who, like David King, were prepared to take risks and introduce community care in their own areas, without waiting for official endorsement, the concept would have been even slower to take hold. It was essential to show that it was possible to transfer services from hospital to community and—although the policy is based on better care, not saving of money—that it is financially feasible. The success of the pioneering community mental health care services established in Devon proved beyond doubt that they *could* be provided, and that the people who use them find them infinitely preferable to the large old institutions they replaced.

The trend towards providing care for mentally ill people in the community has not been a purely British phenomenon, but is part of a world wide movement. As Britain becomes more involved in Europe, it is interesting to recall the statement at the end of the Council of Europe's Second Conference of European Heath Ministers in 1985 'reaffirming the importance of mental health promotion and the prevention of disorders as essential components of a comprehensive policy .... area based and geared to the needs and active participation of those interested and of the public'.

The World Health Organisation and other international bodies have acknowledged that Britain has taken the lead in finding acceptable alternatives to mental hospital care. This book, describing the actual experience of moving away from an outdated institution-based system, to one more suited to the needs of the 21st century, offers inspiration as well as practical knowledge to the many places (in Britain as well as in other countries) where large mental hospitals continue to provide the main form of care.

EDITH MORGAN
*Founder President,*
*European Regional Council*
*World Federation for Mental Health.*

# CONTENTS

*The bottom line: community care is better
value for money than mental hospitals, 100.*

## APPENDICES

# INTRODUCTION

After more than a century of service the Victorian mental hospitals have reached the end of their useful lives. For many years the numbers of patients in them have slowly dwindled and in consequence, costs have risen but the same cannot be said for the standards of service. Plans to replace the mental hospitals by a new style of service characterised as 'community care' (a mix of local domiciliary, ambulatory and short stay hospital care), first mooted in the 60s, have failed to materialise because of lack of money and the conviction to see them come to pass. This lack of resolve stems in part from perceived problems in the alternative to the mental hospitals for community care, as it is currently envisaged, does not provide all the answers. Yet the mental hospitals have had their day and it is time for the world to move on and find, by trial and error, better styles of service paid for in large part by the resources now locked up in the hospitals.

This is an account of the work of many hundreds of people in one corner of England. So far as we know, they achieved a first in the U.K., or—come to that—anywhere in the world. Their achievement was to develop comprehensive community mental health and mental handicap services by using the resources released from the closure of old mental hospitals. They were motivated by one well intentioned and driving purpose: to make a reality of the concept that people with mental illness and mental handicap should no longer be excluded from ordinary life but share in it. Nineteenth century ideas had created institutions designed to separate such people from society. Devon had its full share of these institutions and now, thanks to the efforts of the people who once worked in them, the remote and isolated hospitals have been replaced by a set of comprehensive services designed to meet the needs of their clients, and based in the communities in which they live.

I was privileged to work with them in a position which called for imagination and leadership. But my job was no more important than any other, for we were all inter-dependent. Nobody was more important than another, for without every individual contribution it would not have happened.

The events to be related are an example of ordinary people deciding of their own accord to get on with things. At a time when ordinary people have decided to overturn massive empires, it may seem of comparatively slight importance. But it shows what can be done when people choose to take the matter of reform into their own hands.

I have written this as a tribute to all those who took part. Names have been excluded, for it would be impracticable to include them all. More difficult than that, would be to attempt an assessment of their individual contributions.

The experience was one of the happiest and most fulfilling times of my life, and I believe it was so for others too. The joy of it all was to work with so many people united in a single purpose. To each and every one of them I am grateful for the experience shared. That would be enough, but there was the added pleasure of the response from all those we helped to release from the hospitals. They have shown how wrong it was for them to have been there and how much they have appreciated their new lease on life.

The long time it has taken me to complete the task led me to think that Devon's contribution would be swept aside by other examples and stirring events, as 'care in the community', with its implication of recycling the mental hospitals, became a national movement of giant proportions. That has not been the case—more's the pity. So the story still needs to be told to encourage others.

The account is simply my view of what took place, why and how. Others who took part will have a different perspective. So big a medley of projects calls for other accounts and these will be as reliable as mine, for in history there is no one complete statement. I hope that at least one of these takes a more 'nuts and bolts' approach for those readers who will be disappointed that my broad brush does not include the detailed 'how to do it' instructions.

I am most grateful to Michael Ashley-Miller, of the Nuffield Provincial Hospital Trust, for his insistence that I should write it—and his patience in waiting for me to complete the task. Jeanette Crossley and Kate Smiley have put up with my delays and ordered the sentences and paragraphs so that it makes a coherent account. I thank them both.

Edith Morgan has been a constant source of support through the years of change and I am pleased she has chosen to write a foreword.

I hope that this account will give encouragement and ideas to anyone embarking on a similar task. I hope also that it will help those who are anxious about the disappearance of the mental hospitals to understand that the exercise was not to reduce or cheapen services, nor to cast people in need of care into an uncaring society—but to improve matters for them.

DAVID KING

*Auckland* *February 1991*

# 1

# The what and why of recycling

> There they stand, isolated, majestic, imperious, brooded over by the gigantic water tower, unmistakable and daunting out of the countryside—the asylums which our forefathers built with such solidity.

This is how Enoch Powell described the Victorian mental hospitals in 1962 during his period of office as Minister of Health. He is popularly associated with the first official indications that the mental hospitals would wither and die. But such predictions were premature, for in the intervening years very few of the asylums have closed.

## TWO TYPES OF MENTAL HOSPITAL: AND EVOLVING TERMINOLOGY

During their long spell of service since the 1840s the hospitals and their resident populations have undergone many changes of name, according to the current fashion.

The buildings were known as 'institutions' and 'asylums' before they became 'hospitals'. Those admitted were 'inmates', 'patients', 'residents' and recently, 'clients' or 'customers'.

Some of the hospitals were designed for the care and treatment of people with a mental illness, a condition acquired and more or less amenable to alteration. What started as 'lunacy', and became 'mental illness' and 'psychiatric illness' is now generally included in the description 'mental health'.

1

The other kind of hospital was for those who were considered to lack the mental ability for ordinary development. Such people have been described as 'idiots', the 'mentally subnormal', more recently 'mentally or intellectually handicapped', and now 'people with learning disability'. In this book, I use the terms which seem most appropriate for the period being described.

Each type of hospital admitted not only its own category of patient. There were often people with learning difficulties in mental illness hospitals, and, although not so commonly, the converse. Vagueness of diagnosis meant that people with various conditions were at one time or another admitted to the hospitals. There were also inmates with physical disabilities, or head injuries, moral delinquents, and vagrants.

Prior to the 1960s, once admitted to one of these hospitals, a patient was usually there for life.

## MODERNISATION PROGRAMMES PREDICTED HOSPITAL CONTRACTION THEN CLOSURE

In the 1960s, the role of mental illness and mental subnormality hospitals was changing rapidly. New attitudes to care and treatment, and new drugs affecting behaviour, both meant that much more could be offered to patients on a daily basis. Hospital residence was no longer a pre-requisite for psychiatric care. There were high hopes that community care would replace the old hospital system.

Mr Powell instituted a modernisation programme for all hospitals, published in January 1962. The Department of Health's *Hospital Plan for England and Wales* envisaged major changes in the mental illness hospitals. Between 1960 and 1975 the bed provision would roughly halve from 3·3 to 1·8 beds per 1000 population. 'A large number of the old hospitals would in the course of time be abandoned,' said the Plan.

For Exeter the Plan predicted that the number of psychiatric hospital beds would fall from 2350 in 1960 to 1300 in 1975. The prediction was not far off the mark for in 1975 the actual number of beds was 1314, with a daily occupancy of 1100 patients.

The Plan was less clear about the eventual fate of mental subnormality hospitals, though it indicated they too would reduce in size. In 1960 there were 1711 hospital beds of this kind in Exeter; the Plan anticipated 1163 by 1975, a reduction of 30 per cent. Hospital statistics show that in 1975 there were still 1466 beds —considerably in excess of the prediction—though the average number occupied daily, 1245, was close to the original estimate.

Since 1962, mental hospitals of both types have reduced in size, as the Plan said they would—but they have gently melted like icebergs, reducing in scale but not disappearing. The much heralded demise has not come to pass and most of the old mental hospitals still 'stand...daunting out of the countryside'.

## WHY MENTAL HOSPITALS DID NOT GENERALLY CLOSE

To achieve a purpose there has to be a clear idea of the goal, a method for achieving it, the means to effect the change, and, above all, the will to do it.

The will has certainly been lacking for the closure of the mental hospitals. The public has found it difficult to understand why people whose condition once made it necessary for them to be shut away are now considered fit to be in society. A common reaction is that there are enough problems on the streets without adding to them. Families with mentally ill or handicapped members fear the disappearance of the hospitals as a transfer back to them of the full burden of care and support. They have also seen examples of patients being discharged to boarding houses more squalid than the hospitals, and, worse than that, simply being cast on to the streets to live 'rough'. Hospital staff have also resisted the change for a variety of reasons, and not least to protect their livelihoods.

All these groups tend to see the movement to close hospitals as the work of an alliance of ideological zealots and unscrupulous administrators who do not have the best interests of patients or their families foremost in mind. This lack of enthusiasm from community, family, and staff has, no doubt, influenced the intentions of politicians for whom the whole subject is a bed of nails.

The other factor slowing progress is the absence of clear alternatives to hospital care—knowing what to do, and how to move from the old to the new. There have been few examples to follow and little evidence of success to encourage others to follow.

Establishing these new patterns has been all the more difficult since community care runs counter to the trend in most other secondary health care services—the past thirty years has seen the increasing transfer of fragmented services into ever larger centralised hospitals.

The common complaint that progress has been slow because of a lack of funds is only partly true. There are pockets of progress around the country which indicate that it can be done—the required ingredient is the will to get on with it. Very few people are interested to improve these services and claim lack of money as a convenient excuse for lack of activity.

## COMMUNITY CARE PROGRAMMES
## IN EXETER ENABLED THE
## MENTAL HOSPITALS CLOSURE

A national policy, *Better Services for the Mentally Ill* (Cmnd 6233), for the introduction of locally based hospital and community psychiatric services was promulgated in 1975. Like the 1962 *Hospital Plan*, it envisaged the gradual replacement of the old, specialist, psychiatric hospitals. This policy initiative was not followed through with a national implementation plan: which explains why so little has changed in the past 15 years. There has been some progress, but it has been the result of local interest and initiative to get on with the job. Exeter is one of the very few places where this has happened. This book is an account of a deliberate move there from the old isolated mental hospital system, to a range of small and local, user friendly services, and how the resources released from the old were recycled to pay for the new.

In 1975, there were in Exeter eleven mental illness and mental handicap hospitals, with beds for 3000 patients. Now, in 1990, the transformation of services is almost complete (see Tables 1 and 2). Six hospitals have closed, and three more have changed from being long-stay residential institutions to providing short-stay and day services. In place of the hospitals, local networks cater for the individual needs of the people they serve. Whereas the hospitals served the whole population of Devon but were centralised in one part of it, today's new services are spread throughout the county.

Initially, the aim was to improve the hospitals. But it gradually became clear that this was not the best use of time and resources for it perpetuated a redundant and inappropriate system for ever fewer recipients, while the majority of people in need remained with little help in the community.

In Exeter, a new service was designed, the will to achieve it was kindled, and the resources were drawn largely from existing sources, principally from the hospitals themselves.

TABLE 1. *Mental illness hospitals in Exeter*

| HOSPITAL | NUMBER OF BEDS | | |
|---|---|---|---|
| | 1960 | 1990 | |
| Exminster | 1606 | – | (Closed 1986) |
| Digby | 583 | – | (Closed 1990) |
| Wonford | 160 | 120 | (Exeter District Acute Unit) |
| Hostels for people with long term mental health problems | | 90 | |
| 9 Units for confused elderly people | | 200 | |
| | 2349 | 410 | |

TABLE 2. *Hospitals for people with learning disability*

| HOSPITAL | NUMBER OF BEDS | | |
|---|---|---|---|
| | 1960 | 1990 | |
| Starcross | 758 | – | (Closed 1986) |
| Langdon* | 520 | – | (Closed 1990) |
| Hawkmoor | 140 | – | (Opened in 1972 and closed in 1987) |
| St Mary's Axminster | 156 | – | (Closes 1990) |
| Western, Crediton | 102 | – | (Closed 1989) |
| Franklyn | 55 | 6 | (Closes early 1991) |
| Stoke Lyne | 55 | 6 | (Closes early 1991) |
| Home of Good Shepherd | 65 | | |
| Local Support Units | – | 44 | Adult |
| | | 16 | Children |
| | 1711 | 72 | |

*There is now a forensic psychiatric service at Langdon with 60 beds which serves the countries of Devon and Cornwall.

These tables give no account of developments in the other three Devon and Cornwall health districts funded by the hospital closures in Exeter.

# 2

# Consumer satisfaction: the proof of the pudding

## THE CONSUMERS REPORT THEY PREFER COMMUNITY BASED CARE

This chapter records the views of the most important people of all—the consumers of the services. Their vote has been a universal 'thumbs up' in favour of community solutions. Nobody I talked to would like to return to institutional care. Many do not want to talk about the institutional experience, shutting it out so as to forget the miserable past. When so many people who have never known life in a mental hospital are critical of care in the community, it is as well to keep in mind the opinion of those who have.

My interest and enthusiasm for reforming psychiatric and mental handicap services have been sustained by all the former hospital residents who have found more fulfilling lives in the community than they had ever known in the institutions. Although hospital care was supposed to be beneficial, release from hospital has been as good as a cure for so many who were thought to be beyond hope.

I have found that a wide spectrum of former patients from mental illness and mental handicap hospitals can derive benefit from more normal existence, including people with so-called severe conditions.

Sadly, there are still powerful voices arguing that life in mental hospitals is a happy existence—probably because of no direct experience with them. Certainly, the hospital offers a better alternative to a homeless, unsupported existence. But there are other, better alternatives as this book will show.

## SANDHILL PARK'S
## FIRST GROUP HOME IS A SUCCESS

My introduction to the business of moving long-term patients out of hospital to an ordinary life in the community came twenty years ago in Somerset. I was on the administrative staff for a group of hospitals and the head office was located in one of them, Sandhill Park, a mental handicap hospital. It was my first experience of working in such a hospital and it had never occurred to me that there could be patients there who had no need of the place because they were perfectly able, with varying degrees of assistance, to lead ordinary lives outside.

Members of the nursing staff soon convinced me that there were six men and women all diagnosed as mentally handicapped, whose abilities had been grossly under-estimated, and who would be capable of conducting their own lives. It happened that the hospital authority owned a large terrace house in a town ten miles away. The house had once been used as staff accommodation for nurses at the local general hospital but in recent years it had lain vacant, a target for vandals and a nuisance to the neighbours. We agreed that I would get it furnished and decorated, and the nurses would train the patients to shop and keep house. Somerset Social Services offered to support the group and give whatever help they needed in their new life.

The group, then in their 40s and 50s, were life-long inmates of the mental handicap hospital, and this would be their first taste of freedom. Most of them had been admitted to the hospital as children, and since then had left it only to work outside 'on parole' from the institution. The initial diagnosis of mental subnormality had never been re-assessed—they were life-long victims of an outdated diagnostic system.

Sandhill Park's first group home, opened in 1973, was a success. Indeed, within a short time the only remarkable thing about it was that anyone should ever have thought it remarkable.

I was very keen to see how they were getting on, and called in one day. As I knocked at the door, I realised that it was wrong to be visiting uninvited, though I would have walked through their wards at the hospital without giving it a thought. I asked how they were faring with the neighbours and was told, 'The old lady next door is a bit wary of us, but we have offered to prune her roses and if we help in the garden, she'll soon get to know us.'

It was a depressing thought for anyone aware of the over-crowded conditions and institutional lifestyle in hospital, that these six people and many others like them had been ensnared in a regimented institutional existence when they could be enjoying a more independent life in the community. More group homes were established for Sandhill Park residents and the idea was taken up by staff at the neighbouring mental illness hospital, Tone Vale, where there were also people ready for the change. It is shameful that even today there are still large numbers of residents in mental handicap and mental illness hospitals around the world who could share in and benefit from this freedom.

## PHYSICAL HANDICAP AND AGE ARE NOT ARGUMENTS AGAINST COMMUNITY CARE

The general public is unfortunately unaware of the vast numbers of people who were admitted to hospital for the slightest reasons, and who have remained institutionalised for most of their lives. Sometimes I am told that it is heartless to uproot them after so many years. I once put this proposition to a physically disabled lady who had spent her whole life in a vast mental handicap institution in the suburbs of London—though she was not mentally handicapped. She always seemed to be smiling and content. Wouldn't she rather finish her days in the hospital community she knew so well? After a moment's pause she said, 'Oh no! I would love to know what it is to have my own front door. Just give me the chance'.

I hope she was given the opportunity like another of my acquaintances who was similarly afflicted. Physically but not mentally disabled, he had spent the first fifty years of his life in a mental handicap hospital, but did manage to get out in the end. I encountered him over the years when visiting the crowded ward in which he lived, and on each occasion he would ask whether he could move into the community. But with his severe physical disabilities, it seemed impossible. He was among the last to leave the hospital, and the first two places he tried did not work out. But when I last met him in Exeter, at a carol service in the cathedral, he had found the happiness he sought for so long. He shares a flat with two others, and their support comes from former hospital staff. He told me that the name we had known him by for all those years was not the one he was christened with. When he was first admitted to hospital there was another boy in the children's ward with the same name, so to avoid confusion they gave the newcomer another name, which stayed with him nearly all his life.

It does appear that you cannot be too old to enjoy greater freedom. I knew two ladies who at 86 enjoyed their new life in a well run and homely hostel, after 60 years in a mental hospital where they had originally been admitted for 'excitability.' Another of Exeter's community hostels houses a group of Polish ex-soldiers who had been in hospital since the war. They are old men now, but had they been rehabilitated earlier they may have found the spirit to find jobs and live independently.

## COMMUNITY RE-HOUSING REDUCES THE STRAIN ON FAMILIES

There is a mistaken notion that hospital care was the best help for families. It stems from the idea that the disabled or troubled child should be put away, out of sight and out of mind of his or her family so that they could get on with their lives. But families who kept in touch with their son or daughter in hospital often found the experience harrowing. There were people I met who travelled a round trip of 180 miles from Cornwall to visit a son in one of Exeter's mental handicap hospitals. He was there because of unreliable and occasionally violent conduct. When he went to live in a group home closer to his family in Cornwall he calmed down. His family discovered that the former aggressive outbursts were caused by his embarrassment at having to receive them on a hospital ward, and his vexation at being returned to it after a happy day's outing in their company.

The confused elderly formed a very large group of patients in the Exeter psychiatric hospitals. Removing them a long way from home to big hospital wards was hardly likely to reduce their confusion. It was also a big step for their family, usually the wife or husband, to abandon them to the institution. Now, in the Exeter district, there is a range of local services—support at home, day, and short-term residential care as well as the opportunity for carers to learn from each other in support groups.

## HELP AT LAST FOR FAMILIES WHO DECLINED TO HOSPITALISE THEIR RELATIVE

The examples above have all concerned people moving out of hospital. But, not all the people who needed help would come near the hospitals, such was their dread of life in them. Many families took on the full burden of care rather than 'put away' their son or daughter. For them there was no help until the advent of community services.

In the days when there was no alternative to the hospital in Exeter, I was taken to visit an elderly widow who looked after her middle-aged son, a man with learning disabilities. For many years she had been unable to take a holiday, though she would have liked one—but the only respite care we offered was a large and unlovely hospital. She would not enjoy her holiday knowing her son would be miserable on a ward of thirty men in conditions totally alien to life at home. Today, he would be offered a range of opportunities for short-term or respite care. And chances are that the man would be living an independent life in a group home or hostel, with his own room and the support which formerly could only be given by his aged mother.

Another family had a son at home, a young man with learning disabilities who could be a trouble to himself and his family. But they too were deeply unhappy about the Hobson's choice: no alternative other than admission to a large hospital. Being forthright people they frequently criticised the services in public to spur us to improve. I often had to explain and defend our position to the press and at public meetings. It was an uncomfortable task. Today, they are among the first to defend the record of the health and social services in Exeter.

The persistent concern of parents who take on the care of a disabled son or daughter is what will happen when they die. The prospect of alternatives to hospital care is a great consolation.

A friend whose son had schizophrenia told me that he refused the only life we could offer of long-stay hospital care. But as there was nothing else, they had no help at all. In many families lives are disrupted by sons and daughters suffering from this condition. It is a problem with no easy solution. However, today a specialist team is on hand to help with a range of living and occupational alternatives, and support for families.

## EVEN SEVERE CASES WERE SUCCESSFULLY REHOUSED IN THE COMMUNITY

A common argument for the status quo that I have heard for the last twenty years is that the days of the easy discharges are over, that we are now down to the folk who really need hospital care. I can't accept that excuse. It's a matter of providing the appropriate degree of community support.

For a long time we could envisage no alternative to hospital care for those people with learning disabilities and a propensity for self mutilation and uncontrolled behaviour. But now even they are living in ordinary terraced houses, their behaviour and quality of life improved beyond recognition.

There remain some groups for whom shorter or longer stays in hospital will be necessary, to protect against danger to themselves and to others. But the existence of these relatively small groups does not justify the retention of so many mental hospitals, or the continued incarceration of countless people who would prefer community living and, given the opportunity, will make a success of it.

## COMMUNITY CARE MEANS WORK, LEISURE, AND SOCIAL OPPORTUNITIES TOO

Of course, much more has to be done than simply providing a roof for former patients. Work, leisure, and social activities are all necessary for effective integration into the community. Creating these opportunities is hard work, but far more rewarding than trying to make a normal life in the artificial conditions of a hospital. In some instances, former patients have themselves been closely involved in the organisation of activities. In Exeter ex-patients run a social club where people can call in for a game of cards and a cup of tea at the weekends. Time can hang heavy on Sundays and so the club is greatly appreciated. Another group of former patients offers its services to the public as interior decorators.

For large numbers of people, the proof of the pudding has been in the eating. It has been a great joy in so many cases to see the benefits of release from hospital transforming a regimented life into one in which the individuals choose their own routines. Likewise, it has been good to see those people who would not accept hospital care obtaining some help, often for the first time, from the community services.

Reforming psychiatric services is probably harder, more unpopular, and more controversial than any other activity associated with health services. But I know of no more rewarding and fulfilling work. Helping hospital staff and residents to a new life, and watching them develop and flourish, have been the greatest bonus.

# 3

# Mental hospitals v community care: a brief history

In the Spring of 1986, I took part in a debate organised by the Royal College of Psychiatrists. The topic was whether or not to replace the mental hospitals with community services. The hospital psychiatrists voted over-whelmingly against 'care in the community' on the grounds that the hospitals offered the needy a safe haven or 'asylum'. Benefits of the old mental hospital system are often extolled—a calm and protected environment, a sanctuary, or 'asylum' in the true meaning of the word. But memory is selective, so we should trace the history of the mental hospitals to see what quality of asylum they have actually provided for the past 150 years.

## THE MENTAL HOSPITAL SYSTEM: PART 1. 1840–1900

### AN ALTERNATIVE TO THE WORKHOUSES

Victorian society agonised over how to support those members of society who were too poor to maintain themselves. The result was a policy based on 'indoor' rather than 'outdoor' relief. Yes, there would be help but to receive it meant leaving home and entering an institution—there would be no cash hand-outs to sustain the poor in the community, because the irresponsible could so easily abuse the money to maintain their feckless way of life. So help would carry the penalty and stigma of institutional life, an incentive to encour-

15

age the 'undeserving poor' to fend for themselves rather
than face the rigours of a deliberately designed uncongenial existence.

Even the tough minded Victorian recognised a snag
in this policy of encouraging self help. The squalor of
the workhouse may have been appropriate for the
'undeserving poor', those who could be stimulated to
fend for themselves. But it put an unfair imposition on
the 'deserving poor', those unable to cope on their own,
a group which included 'lunatics' and 'defectives'. So
the mental hospitals were built to offer better accommodation than the workhouses provided. However, the
methods of administration made these hospitals very
different institutions from our concept of a hospital
today.

### COMPULSORY ASYLUM

Firstly, the style of care required compulsory isolation
from society. Political asylum has a long and distin-
guished history, and mental asylum may seem to be an
extension of its benefits. But the two differ in a fundamental way. The former is a course voluntarily adopted
by a persecuted individual, but the latter is a remedy
imposed on individuals against their will.

For about 120 years, from about 1840 to 1960, 'lunatics' and 'defectives' were regarded as sub-normal and
sub-human. Official policy's aim was to bring them
under control in a separate world designed for their
care and protection where treatment and rehabilitation
could take place. The mental hospitals were created for
this purpose and every local authority was obliged to
provide asylum for its pauper lunatics.

The Lunacy and Mental Deficiency Acts required
constables, relieving officers and overseers with knowledge of a 'lunatic' wandering in their district or parish
to apprehend and deliver the person to a Justice of the
Peace. 'Defectives' and 'lunatics' who escaped from an
institution could be apprehended and returned without
warrant.

## ARBITRARY SELECTION OF INMATES

Secondly, the hospitals opened their gates to all kinds of people. Because the methods of diagnosis were inadequate and arbitrary, a wide range of people were included.

In the last century, the selection of cases appropriate for admission to hospital was a matter for local determination, although the Lunacy and Mental Deficiency Acts, dating from 1845, gave general advice. At Royal Western Counties Hospital, Starcross, a policy was initiated in 1879, to select only those 'cases' possessing sufficient intelligence 'to warrant the hope that permanent improvement could be effected'. The lowest 'types of idiocy' were not deemed suitable for admission. Reading between the lines, it seems likely that poor families were able to offer to the hospital authorities those children they either did not want or could not afford to maintain, and Starcross selected the fittest and most intelligent of them.

These policies of keeping the streets clear of 'undesirables' and receiving the unwanted children of the poor meant that for a hundred years, all sorts of people were admitted to the mental hospitals for the remainder of their life-time. People with learning or physical disabilities, moral reprobates, vagrants, people with mental health problems, and social misfits were all indiscriminately admitted to both kinds of institution. Many normal people became trapped in the system.


## BEHAVIOUR CONTROL: 'INSTITUTIONALISATION'

Thirdly, the regime conditioned inmates to the disciplines of a completely regimented or institutional life.

The disciplined life induced a condition known as 'institutionalisation' which afflicted both staff and patients. Its characteristics were a slavish adherence to the routines of the hospital and a loss of independent thought and action—hardly surprising when the institution left no aspect of life untouched. Male and female patients were nursed in separate wards . . . sometimes in separate wards (sometimes in separate hospitals) and only met for dances and social events conducted under the strictest supervision. The time of waking and lights out, the work to be done and when, even the selection of lettuce to replace cabbage for lunch during the summer, were all matters for decision by the Medical Superintendent, whose rule was absolute.

When, much later, the hospitals assumed their rehabilitation role, critics became concerned about the results of 'institutionalisation'. It was then regarded as an unfortunate and unintended side effect, not unlike wound infection after a surgical operation. But, in reality, it had been a fundamental feature and requirement of the former mental hospital system, necessary to control the behaviour of large numbers of people denied freedom and shut away in artificial communities.

The hospital regimes described above were intended for the systematic stripping of individuality, and suppression of any ambition to have it restored. How else could people be made to accept the conditions and stop trying to escape? Society condoned a system for the total control of inmates and their life-time removal from ordinary society. It was deliberate, well intentioned and unbelievably effective. It was too pervading a feature of the hospitals even though they had changed their basic purpose. They were not adaptable for their new rehabilitation role.

# THE MENTAL HOSPITAL SYSTEM
## PART 2: 1900–1960

### INCREASING NUMBERS ADMITTED FOR LIFE

Ever increasing numbers of people were admitted to the hospitals during the first half of the twentieth century, and once admitted, there was little chance or expectation of discharge and return to ordinary society.

At the outbreak of the First World War, 13 staff at Starcross Hospital were called up for service. A number of patients were given the temporary rank of assistant, to fill the gap left. A booklet published by the Hospital Management Committee (the forerunner of Health Authorities) in 1964 entitled *Royal Western Countries— The First Hundred Years* records:

The lads rose splendidly to the occasion and proved themselves worthy of the trust reposed in them.

But there is no further comment. No surprise is expressed that such able people were inmates, nor is any mention made of their subsequent progress—whether, having proved themselves, they went off to find jobs outside the hospital after the war. The chances are that they once more resumed the role of patients.

Many hospital residents were allowed out of the hospitals to perform menial tasks as servants in other institutions, schools, and farms, or to work as labourers. They were very poorly paid, and if they became ill or fell out with their employers, they were re-admitted at once to the hospital. An eloquent example of hospitalisation being a life-long condition, rather than for active treatment and rehabilitation, was told to me by a doctor who for a short time in the 1960s worked as a locum medical officer in Wiltshire at Roundway Hospital (mental illness). Every patient had an annual medical check-up. In the records of one lady he examined was the note made by a previous doctor some years earlier: 'Not so well this year'.

### OVERCROWDING WAS OFFICIALLY CONDONED

The constant admission of ever more patients for life-long care meant that the numbers of people in hospital grew inexorably. Though there seems to have been some attempt to develop more mental handicap hospitals in the 1920s and 1930s, there was an easier and apparently acceptable solution. This was simply to fit the extra numbers into the same space. When the Board of Control Commissioners (the national governing body) paid its annual visit to Exminster Hospital in 1940 it reported serious over-crowding for the 1474 patients in residence. The hospital had been built to house 440. Yet two years later the same number of men were still there, 560, and many more women, 993 compared to 911 in 1940, (a mysterious and unexplained war-time change) and staff numbers were down (Table 3). Admittedly it was war-time, but this is not recorded as an excuse for the over-crowding. The Board of Control Commissioners' report included in the 1942 *Annual Report of the Devon Mental Hospital* runs as follows: 'Dr Allan (the Medical Superintendent) has dealt with the over-crowding problem successfully, and we do not think any possible re-arrangement would be an improvement.'

The Board evidently did not expect high standards. In 1940 they had commented that the installation of a basin fitted for hot and cold water 'would be a real boon' for the nursing staff on a ward used to house senile and bedridden women. In the course of that visit they report having seen all the patients in residence: ' . . . though we received remarkably few complaints, none of them, in our opinion, justifiable.'

TABLE 3. *Patient staff numbers—Exminster Hospital*

| YEAR | | DAY STAFF | NIGHT STAFF |
|------|------|------|------|
| | MALE PATIENTS | | |
| 1940 | 563 | 77 | 9 |
| 1942 | 560 | 66 | 9 |
| | FEMALE PATIENTS | | |
| 1940 | 911 | 93 | 17 |
| 1942 | 993 | 91 | 15 |

With a war to fight and the official inspectorate content with conditions society could forget the mental hospitals. The interesting thing is that it was after the war that the worst excesses of over-crowding occurred. But in the 1960s there was an explosion of public outrage when the complacency of the authorities was finally revealed in a series of public enquiries.

# CARE IN THE COMMUNITY V HOSPITAL IMPROVEMENT: 1960–1990

## *DECREASING HOSPITAL POPULATIONS FOLLOWED THE 1959 MENTAL HEALTH ACT*

The 1959 Mental Health Act helped change social attitudes to psychiatric care, removing the need for compulsory detention save in exceptional cases. Until this time the statistics for Exminster Hospital showed that more than 80 per cent of the patients were certified —detained involuntarily.

The change was of major importance—but like all significant innovation, it took time to have practical effect. At first there was paper change only for one large mental handicap hospital in the south of England. As soon as the new law was passed, 900 of the 1000 residents were freed from compulsory detention and became 'informal patients' still resident at the hospital but free to go if they wished. One of them, taking advantage of this new freedom, decided to leave the hospital—but returned a day or two later, tired and hungry. The others who had been freed from compulsory detention made no attempt to leave. Life went on much as before, except that grandiose plans to expand the hospital were abandoned.

Nevertheless, hospital populations which had increased for more than a century began to reduce. But this mysterious turn in the tide was not yet due to the impact of community care programmes.

## *HOSPITAL SCANDALS EXPOSED CONTINUED OVERCROWDING*

The neglect and the over-crowding of the mental hospitals reached a peak at the end of the 1950s.

In 1958 a ward in Exminster Hospital housed 118 patients in such conditions that the beds had to be pushed together at night so that they would fit into the available space. Wire baskets hung beneath the beds into which the day-time clothes were bundled. This is only one example of wards in which there was no room to move between beds, no proper storage space for clothes, and primitive lavatories and bathrooms, all of which meant that patients had no privacy at all. Moreover, in the exercise yard, patients were tied together in groups of three to stop them wandering off.

In such conditions, it is not surprising that standards of patient care in some hospitals fell far short of the mark. This came to light during the 1960s and 1970s in a number of public reports and there was public outcry and a call for action. A set of minimum hospital standards was introduced, and increased funding was allocated to improve the hospitals.

### MORE PATIENTS DISCHARGED IN AN ATTEMPT TO 'SANITISE' THE MENTAL HOSPITALS

Though extra funds were made available they did not allow expansion of the hospital facilities to cater for all the patients in them. So ways had to be found to reduce the patient numbers, thereby enabling the existing wards and departments to be upgraded and staffing ratios increased. Vast numbers who did not need hospital care were discharged. But it was to an impoverished life in boarding houses, because the extra resources were devoted only to hospital improvement, and there was no build-up of support services in the community.

One social worker in Exeter was responsible for the relocation of many hundreds of patients into boarding houses and cheap hotels in the late 1960s and early 1970s. To her great credit, she stayed in touch with them and does so today. But in Devon and many other parts of the country, no adequate provision was made to provide all the other necessary provisions for this mass exodus. Nor was this significant change in policy explained to a public increasingly concerned as it saw forlorn people wandering the streets with time on their hands and nowhere to go. The reduction of hospital populations at that time, far from marking a growth in community care, was a desperate scramble to sanitise hospital conditions. Patients were tipped out of hospitals to a community with no adequate support services.

Unfortunately, the public could only conclude that this sudden appearance of large numbers of former hospital patients was the meaning of 'care in the community', and naturally they condemned it outright.

One popular explanation for the discharge of patients is that it was all made possible by the introduction of new behaviour modifying drugs. These had their part to play, but for many former patients, particularly those from the mental handicap hospitals, the less crowded conditions and greater freedom reduced their reliance on these drugs.

Oddly enough, the hospitals which had been under threat of closure found themselves with a new lease of life. Staff and their trade unions found that the public opinion which had passively condoned the old order, now condemned them for allowing it to happen. Hospital staff found themselves in the dock for doing the job that society had so recently condoned. Understandably, they went on the defensive.

The Department of Health specified 'minimum standards' of patient accommodation in the hospitals. These were intended to improve conditions and resulted in better staff/patient ratios and fewer patients on every ward.

Instead of progress being made towards 'care in the community', attention was focussed on increasing the resources invested in hospitals, which were catering for fewer and fewer people.

### LIFE CYCLE OF EXMINSTER HOSPITAL

The effects of the admission/discharge policies described in the foregoing sections can be seen in the following diagram which shows the varying numbers of in-patients in one hospital, Exminster, during its 130 year history. 100 years to grow from some 300 patients to 1600 in 1955. 30 years to reduce and finally shut its doors, and for most of this time no conscious policy for hospital closure. I can offer no explanation for the stabilisation and decline in numbers between 1895 and 1925. It would be fascinating to know the reasons.

*In-patient numbers at Exminster 1849-1985*

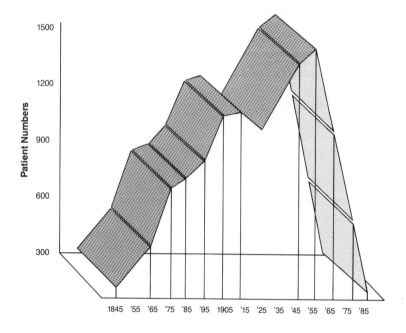

*THE MISSING ELEMENT:*
*INSUFFICIENT PRIORITY GIVEN TO MENTAL HEALTH POLICY*
*AND ITS IMPLEMENTATION*

If mental health policy had been given the same priority over the last 30 years as in Victorian times, then people of similar vision, stature, and energy might have been involved. Mental health policy has, however, been left on a back burner—with occasional interventions by Secretaries of State of the calibre of Richard Crossman, but largely in the hands of ever changing Ministers in the House of Lords.

The big mental hospitals have no long-term future, but they lock up both the ideas and resources necessary for change. The Victorian legacy survives. The hospitals were so purpose built that it is impossible for them to be the launching pad for change unless their human and material resources are re-cycled to a different style of service.

Such action requires determination to effect radical change. Exeter's mental hospitals would still be in existence today, but for a conscious policy begun around 1980 to change the nature of psychiatric services—and the will to implement it.

# 4

# Recycling in Exeter: an account of the changes
## 1970–90

## THE SETTING

Devon is a rural county in the South West of England, best known for its cream teas, holiday beaches along the 'English Riviera' and north coast, Dartmoor, picture book villages, historic cities, and rolling agricultural landscape. Its population of about one million people is joined by thousands of tourists during the summer months. It conveniently divides into four areas each with its main urban centre: at the western end is Plymouth, by far the largest city; the holiday resorts of Torbay are in the south; Barnstaple is to the north; and, Exeter, the County Town, lies at the centre of the eastern quarter.

## DEVON'S MENTAL HOSPITALS

Devon started to acquire its mental hospitals in the 1840s. They all provided long-stay institutionalised care, so proximity to home was not a consideration. Moorhaven Hospital (mental illness) was built close to and serves Plymouth. All the others were sited around Exeter, though they served the whole county including communities 60 miles distant from them. Likewise, the mental handicap hospitals were built around Exeter to serve the counties of Devon and Cornwall, the neighbouring county to the west. The hospital services based in Exeter had been organised into two main groups, Exe

Vale (mental illness) and Royal Western Counties (mental handicap).

The largest of the Exe Vale Hospitals was Exminster which takes its name from the village which until recently it dominated. Built to accommodate 440 patients, at one time it housed some 1600 patients, though by the 1970s this number had been halved and it was not until the mid 1980s that there were once more only 400 patients in residence.

Built in 1845 by Charles Fowler, the architect who also designed Dartmoor Prison and Covent Garden Market, Exminster Hospital is a splendid and imposing example of institutional architecture. Centre House, the grand three storey central administrative building with its fine clock tower, stands before and at the apex of a semi-circular arcade from which spring four ward wings fanning out from it. Beyond them, until recently, was another line of buildings, the 'back wards'. These, with associated nurses' homes, staff houses, church, cemetery, laundry, farm, and boiler house were well set in an estate of 100 acres some three miles from the centre of the city on the west bank of the Exe estuary. In its latter years, Exminster contained the acute psychiatric service for the Torbay Health District, many wards for long-stay patients, and even more wards for the care of the confused elderly.

Digby Hospital, Exe Vale's second unit, is on the southern outskirts of the city, and was built in 1886 as the Exeter City asylum. Its 500 beds were largely contained in a line of two storey buildings whose style is faintly Venetian, an impression gained from distant views of the towers with their high pointed roofs standing at each end of the ward block. Villa wards have more recently been added in the extensive grounds.

Wonford House, the third of the Exe Vale Hospitals, started life in 1897 as a private mental institution where it is said the male nurses wore white coats in the morning and changed into dark jackets after lunch. Its grey stone walls, bays and turrets may best be described as Disneyland's idea of a large English country house. It has about 100 beds, and is close to the centre of Exeter. In what were once its gardens and sports-fields has been constructed in 1974 the district general hospital, the Royal Devon and Exeter, which contains most of the consultant hospital services for the Exeter District.

Services for people with mental handicap were pro-vided in eight small units scattered throughout the Exeter District, and two big hospitals. Royal Western Counties Hospital, Starcross, the headquarters, was built in 1864. Although generally considered to be of no architectural merit, Starcross occupied an imposing site on the banks of the Exe estuary ten miles to the south of the city. The greystone four-storied main block, fronted by a magnificent and lovingly tended formal garden, was a familiar landmark to west country travellers on the main railway line to Cornwall which passed Star-cross on the narrow strand between the hospital build-ings and high-water line of the estuary.

Though Starcross had been increased in size to ac-commodate some 500 patients, the need for further expansion resulted in the development of another insti-tution during the 1930s, a few miles farther south. Langdon Hospital is a series of large villa wards, some 10 in all, set in a rolling landscape between the sea and the Haldon Hills. Even this, with its 450 beds, proved insufficient to meet demand, and in the early 1970s Hawkmoor Hospital, a TB sanatorium on the edge of Dartmoor, was used to house the overflow. It was brought into service to help reduce the over-crowded conditions of hospital wards in Exeter and Bristol.

Though nothing matched the initial enthusiasm and energy which brought the hospitals into being, there had been a steady development of their services and plans for the improvement and extension of the buildings in a forlorn effort over the years to try and keep up with the growing numbers of patients. A strategic hospital plan (a concept very much in vogue at the time) was drawn up in 1975 but contained no hint or prospect that within a decade a number of the hospitals would close.

# STIRRINGS OF CHANGE 1970–80

*DEVON AREA HEALTH AUTHORITY ATTEMPTS A POLICY
TO DECENTRALISE PSYCHIATRIC SERVICES*

In 1974, the National Health Service was extensively re-organised to create comprehensive health authorities with responsibilities for hospital and community services. The administrative implications for Devon were that one Area Health Authority was appointed to replace the six former hospital management committees and four community service organisations. Devon was too large for its health services to be managed from one centre, so four health districts (one for each of the county's main population centres) were set up, each with a team of Chief Officers and medical representatives accountable to the Authority for the planning and management of health services. The Exe Vale and Royal Western Counties hospital groups fought hard to maintain their separate status, but it was decided to include them in the Exeter Health Care District—though with strict instructions to its district management team that the two groups, now defined as sectors and each with its own management team, must be afforded maximum delegated responsibility to manage their own affairs and destinies. To ensure there was no shortage of planning, there would also be psychiatric and mental handicap planning teams both at district and county levels. It was a concoction best suited to maintain the status quo, for at any time there were so many different strands of advice in play and awaiting the outcome of tortuous and interminable consultative processes, that the one thing certain not to happen was any significant change.

Nevertheless, the Devon Area Health Authority had an enlightened policy for the decentralisation of psychiatric services. The Authority wanted each of the districts to have local service provision, and a special fund was reserved for this purpose. Hospital conditions were so bad, however, that most of the money was inevitably channelled to their improvement, leaving little to build up the local services. In any case, there was little official enthusiasm within the psychiatric services for decentralisation—the people with the ideas and the energy for change were not at the senior levels of the organisation. It is not unfair to say that community developments were perceived as acts of disloyalty to the mother hospitals (all regarded as 'centres of excellence') whereby easy work was removed from the hospitals, leaving them to cope with the most uncongenial aspects of psychiatric care.

When appointed to Exeter in 1974 as the Exeter District Administrator (chief administrative officer) I became acutely aware of the endless problems and hazards of psychiatric hospital management. Nobody seemed satisfied with the plans to increase staff, or improve conditions. It was impossible to discover who was in charge of the hospitals—though within the Babel of 'multi-disciplinary management' (a concept which gave equal status to various professional and power groups to arrive at decisions through consensus) there was a suspicion that the trade unions had perhaps the most powerful voice.

Hanging over us all was a constant worry that at any time some harassed member of staff or fellow resident might ill-treat an unfortunate patient on the over-crowded wards, necessitating police investigation and the prospect of public scandal. Exeter's services experienced many such complaints from 1974 to 1982, which on two occasions resulted in criminal trial and public enquiry. The hospitals were over-crowded, under staffed, and teeming with unsolved problems.

Yet for more than a decade the closure of all mental hospitals had been predicted by pundits who never explained how it might be achieved. Every new intake of student nurses to the hospitals was told not to expect to spend their whole career there, because the hospitals would one day close. It was not unlike frequent predictions of the end of the world, which after a time are probably treated with scorn. But like grit in the shoe, the problems were constantly nagging at us and demanding attention.

*THE IDEA GELS TO CLOSE EXETER'S MENTAL HOSPITALS*

The turning point came in the late 1970s. In May 1979 a television documentary, two programmes screened on consecutive nights, alleged cruel treatment of patients and scandalous conditions at Rampton Hospital. Rampton is one of the three Special Hospitals managed at that time by the Department of Health for people of dangerous, violent or criminal propensities requiring treatment under conditions of special security. The Secretary of State set up a Rampton Hospital Management Review Team to investigate the management of the hospital. Two of us from Exeter were appointed to the Team.

We expected the worst, but found that much the Review Team criticised at Rampton was equally true of the conditions in most mental hospitals. One solution we considered for Rampton was its closure, an option which was discharged as impracticable. But the seed had been sown.

The advice that if you are surrounded by alligators the answer is to drain the swamp is sound but heroic. However, on my return to Exeter the idea of closing the hospitals seemed to be the best solution for the problems we faced. The alternative was a lifetime's battle trying to reform an unending stream of out of date and inappropriate hospital practices. Ways had to be discovered to put an end to the Victorian institutions and replace them with something better. As Chief Administrator I was in no position to find and fashion the solutions—but I was well placed to spot these staff who did have ideas and to give them every opportunity and encouragement to implement them.

## THE FLOOD TIDE OF CHANGE 1980–90

*A START WITH THE MENTAL HANDICAP HOSPITALS*

The triggers for change were two Re-organisation Working Parties, one for each group of hospitals. In the

Royal Western Counties hospitals the membership comprised psychiatrists, a paediatrician, senior nurses, psychologists, social workers, and administrators. They were guided by two important conclusions which became apparent after long debate.

The first was a view we all came to share—that for people with learning disabilities the hospitals did more harm than good, and that there were better and more practical alternatives for helping them.

The second nugget of information was both more alarming, and at the same time very re-assuring. Helping the working party in its understanding of hospital activity was an operational research scientist who had retired to East Devon after a career in industry. His analyses of both Starcross and Exminster gave insights which strongly influenced the decisions we took. The work at Starcross showed an ever declining patient population which had commenced in the mid 1950s and was relentlessly continuing. Nobody could explain the constant reduction nor could they easily shrug off the possibility that the hospital might one day close because all the patients had been discharged. Possible reasons for this decline are easier to see in hindsight. In the three years from the beginning of 1971 to the end of 1973, the resident population for the mental handicap hospitals reduced by only 13 people, from 1420 to 1407. In the first quarter of 1974 the number was back up to 1416. But by the end of 1975 200 people had been discharged from the hospitals. This significant reduction occurred at the time when the Devon Area Health Authority took over control of the hospital from the former Royal Western Counties Hospital Management Committee. One possible explanation is that the pay of senior staff in hospital management committee had been dependent upon the number of beds (more beds, more pay). In the new order of Health Authorities there was no such linkage affecting the income of health authority staff and therefore no penalty attached to the discharge of patients who did not need to be in the hospitals.

## NEW SERVICES IN THE COMMUNITY FOR MENTAL HANDICAP—AND STARCROSS TO CLOSE

Exeter was fortunate to have a good system in the community for rehousing mentally handicapped people. The reduction in hospital numbers continued throughout the 1970s, until Starcross hospital comprised only 235 beds in 1982. We then asked the operational research scientist to extend the statistical trend to indicate when the hospital would be empty. Since his results showed that was possible by 1988, we decided to plan our own moment for closure, rather than leave it to the fates. It was all heady stuff, even for the small group aware of it, and none of us knew how to break it to the people who depended on the hospital for help and support, and more significantly, to the staff whose very livelihoods would be at stake.

A group of doctors, nurses, clinical psychologists, social workers and administrators, spent two days at hotel in the Haldon Hills overlooking the city to construct a plan for the provision of new services for people with learning disabilities. Away from the hospital we were able to think freely and put aside—for the time being—the shock, dismay, and opposition which would certainly greet our proposals from all quarters. The plan, jointly framed with the local Director of Social Services, envisaged six local teams of skilled and experienced staff stationed throughout the District to set up housing and residential arrangements, short-term care facilities, and day-time occupations for the 1400 or so people with learning disabilities living in the district, 80 per cent of whom were already living in the community. The funds for all these developments would come from hospital closures.

Starcross would be the first hospital to close, and the first at which we held a general meeting to tell the staff. Their response was far less hostile than we had feared. I suspect this was because they had heard similar predictions before, none of which had to come pass. In any case there were still 250 residents in the hospital and a long way to go before it was emptied.

*PLANS FOR NEW COMMUNITY MENTAL HEALTH SERVICES*

A re-organisation Working Party had been formed in 1979 for the Exe Vale hospitals. It was very large, including all the interested professional groups and the principal trade unions. Initially, its work had concentrated upon means to improve living and working conditions in the hospitals. However, it too became concerned with the decentralisation of services to the three client districts, Exeter, Torbay and North Devon. The hospitals had been divided up so that each ward was allocated to one of the districts. In theory, this simplified transferring services from the hospitals because the districts could identify what was theirs, ward by ward.

Happily, the ideas for change were not limited to the straight transfer of existing hospital services. Ideas were developing for community mental health so that in the process of change the nature of the services could be transformed. Many of the staff were excited by this concept. COHSE, the biggest trade union, had concluded, as a result of its own researches, that this kind of arrangement would, sooner or later, replace the hospitals. A majority of us decided that to ignore these movements in the psychiatric hospitals would be to bury our heads in the sand—it would be far better to see what the future had in store and prepare for it. So what started as a focus to improve the hospitals, became a plan to close them and modernise services.

*WORKING TOWARDS THE DECISION TO CLOSE*
*THE MENTAL ILLNESS HOSPITALS*

The death knell for Exminster was sounded by the chairman of the Devon Area Health Authority at the opening of an expensively designed and constructed unit serving the confused elderly people of Dartmouth, a small port and sailing resort 40 miles to the west of Exminster. A ship's bell had thoughtfully been provided to remind the town's elderly former residents of a familiar sound. The chairman rang it to mark the opening.

I had been instrumental two years earlier in promoting the up-grading of the wards. What seemed such a good idea at the time actually turned out to be a bad decision. When it was taken, the wards for the elderly offered the worst accommodation in the hospital, and the need for improvement seemed indisputable. Yet we perpetuated a system which isolated elderly people from their families, when there was little we could do to cure or improve their mental condition. We were providing only a nursing home, and there was no case for it to be so far away from Dartmouth. Further, the project had cost about £750,000, far exceeding initial estimates. When I calculated what it would cost to improve the whole hospital at these prices the total sum was astronomical and I determined this would be the last major building project at Exminster. Fortunately, everyone agreed and thereafter all the capital investment was spent on the provision of local services.

But just as the plan seemed to get a head of steam—having won the support of members and officers of the Devon Area Health Authority—the NHS was, once more, subjected to further re-organisation. Area Health Authorities were out of favour, and each of the districts was to become a Health Authority in its own right. So in Devon, there would be four independent Health Authorities, instead of one. Following their institution, there would be an inevitable restructuring of management, and, perhaps, the appointment of new officers and members who would be less supportive of the plans for care in the community.

So much uncertainty could have been a major setback in the midst of plans to reform the psychiatric services. But in the interregnum the Exeter management team kept the bit between its teeth and, with the co-operation of managers in the other districts, maintained the momentum of reform. Instead of spending the many months of uncertainty gloomily musing on what might come to pass, we decided to use the time to prepare carefully the arrangements needed to implement the reforms, and more importantly, to earmark the people best able to get the job done. Despite a number of alarms, the team weathered this period and was re-appointed, so I continued to be the District Administrator. Our draft proposals were accepted by the new Exeter Health Authority, the other three health authorities in Devon, the County Council and the District Councils. We were ready to implement them when the new Authorities assumed power in 1982.

## THE SUBSTANCE OF THE DECISION

The first key decision was that the central mental hospital services would close and the resources would be equitably shared among the authorities to fund community care.

The second was that the two hospital groups were divided into four management units, each with a specific purpose and positive incentive to commission the new by dismantling the old: a simple process of recycling. In the Exe Vale hospitals (mental health), Exminster comprised one management unit which would close the hospital and open new services in the Torbay and North Devon districts. Digby and Wonford, the other unit would provide the resources for Exeter's community services. These would be established as Digby reduced and closed. In the mental handicap hospital group, Langdon was made a unit for it was envisaged that while the number of residents there would reduce, a need for some mental handicap provision would remain. In the event, there has been no need for its mental handicap services, but this was not known at the time. The second mental handicap unit comprised all the other hospitals. The intention was to relocate the residents in their home communities and recycle the hospital resources to provide local support services. The third step was the appointment of able managers committed to these policies. We were able to find them from within the organisation. Our apparently endless and fruitless meetings had not been in vain after all, for the debate convinced some staff and authority members, who had initially been the most doughty defenders of the hospitals, that the only way to improve the mental health and handicap services to best serve their clients was to scuttle the hospitals.

### UNDERWAY AT LAST!

The period of greatest change was planned to take place between 1982 and 1986, with the build up of local services and the closure of the three main mental hospitals Exminster, Digby and Starcross. And that is precisely what happened. The recycling plan for each hospital was drawn up only in the most general way—a certain number of wards to close and new services to open each year until the hospitals were empty. It was up to each management team to determine the detail of which wards to close, and to design the community services to replace them. Though there was no precedent to guide them, the managers and staff of the hospitals kept to these self imposed time-tables. The staff and clients transferring to the new services were brought together within the hospitals to forge effective units before each move to the community was made.

Closing a ward called for careful discipline—as beds emptied they were removed. When wards closed, managers arranged for them to be locked. This was important for realising the full savings. To help drive home the lesson to any staff who doubted the hospitals would close, we demolished a few wards as soon as they emptied. Later this became counter productive because the building line was necessary to preserve future site development potential. Regular meetings were held with all the staff to keep them informed, and gradually the doubting Thomases, once in the majority, were won over when they saw the impressive accomplishments in the community by their former hospital colleagues.

Convincing everyone it could be done was a continual struggle. It is only fair to record that these doubts plagued even those of us at the centre of things, for none of us had previous experience of converting hospital to community services and there were no examples from elsewhere to follow.

That the battle had been finally won was conveyed to me by two events. The first was a study day at Exminster Hospital at which some Ward Charge Nurses, the key power group of nursing staff, presented ideas for community services for the elderly. That they could approach the changes with enthusiasm was an encouraging signal. The second was a report I received from a frequenter of the Exminster and Starcross pubs used by many hospital staff. His Delphic message was, 'The word is, the family say, the party's over'. Whether or not that means much to the reader, to me it was as significant as the news of the fall of the Bastille.

### FROM THE DISTRICT VIEWPOINT

The job for those of us in the district office was really very clear—to give the managers and staff every support, and to maintain sympathetic and effective channels of communication with all the Health Authorities and many other agencies involved. A key task was also to prepare and maintain reasonable levels of public acceptance of the radical changes.

In 1985 there were more NHS reforms when general management was introduced. In future, the much maligned consensus multi-disciplinary management teams (1974's startling innovation) would be replaced by one manager to whom the various professional groups would be responsible. General management has much to commend it, but Exeter's most radical changes were introduced and brought to pass by the now discredited management culture and style, and before the introduction of general management. Far more important than individual accountability had been the group commitment to a common goal.

After a delay of some months I was promoted from District Administrator to the post of District General Manager in Exeter and was able to continue guiding the programme through the next period of change. This was, however, more a tidying-up operation, since the major part of the reforms had been accomplished. Indeed, my main pre-occupation became the rebuilding of the District General Hospital, so I had very little time to do more than keep a watching brief to see that the new services, once established, were alert and attentive to their changed role.

One of the great criticisms levelled at what we were doing is encapsulated in the term 'trans institutionalisation'. The concern was that the attitudes and customs of the old hospital services were so endemic that in dividing up the hospitals we would do no more than recreate them in smaller form, like someone scattering dandelion seed on the wind. Our hopes that the former hospital staff were capable of change proved fully justified, for the new services were fashioned by the same people who had run the hospitals. In fact the new services have been far more self critical and open to change than almost any other of those for which the Health Authority is responsible, and they continue to grow in their understanding and response to the needs of their clients.

## THE END OF AN ERA: THE MENTAL HOSPITAL SCENE IN 1990

Starcross is demolished, its site filled by a crowded estate of trim executive houses. Yet on the last day of the hospital's existence in June 1985, the gardeners cut the front lawns, out of pride and to leave it in good order. Digby, Exminster and Hawkmoor stand vacant in 1990, and ready for housing estates, shop, and office developments.

The once proud Exminster Hospital, whose problems and complexities once overwhelmed us, stands vacant and for sale. The hospital has been restored to its original shape revealing, once more, Fowler's grand architecture. One amusing footnote is that the demolition contractor—who shaved off all the later additions and extensions—carefully salvaged the excellent build-

ing materials, of which the hospital had been constructed, and found a market in Japan for one consign-
ment of the re-claimed bricks. The re-cycling process is
apparently endless.

All the mental handicap beds have been closed at
Langdon hospital leaving a small forensic psychiatric
unit and Regional Secure Unit. The child and adolescent service, formerly accommodated at Wonford
House, has moved to two elegant town houses and the
hospital continues to provide acute and short-stay
rehabilitation hospital services.

All this stress and change might easily have resulted
in a totally demoralised staff: but not so. They are now
the centre of attention for a stream of visitors eager to
see the new services, and to learn from them how they,
by their own efforts, regenerated psychiatric services
which had fallen on hard times.

Ten years ago anyone predicting this would have
been considered a dreamer or fool. The next chapters
describe the range of services which have replaced the
old hospitals and the mechanics we discovered for
effecting major change.

# 5

# The new patterns

## CONCEPTS OF COMMUNITY CARE

Writing with hindsight it is much easier to clarify the thoughts which guided us seven years ago when the decision was made to close the mental hospitals. They are best described as forces or feelings, for at the time they were by no means clearly articulated and developed concepts. But one thing was clear—a sense that we could do no more and better things for the people we served, and that to stimulate and resource these new approaches it was essential to dispose of the old system.

Closing the old institutions was a relatively simple matter, but replacing them with a comprehensive alternative would be far more difficult. We were anxious to avoid simply decanting the old wine into new and smaller bottles. A slow and piece-meal approach would allow the past to have a strong influence on the future. A swift closure programme would force everyone concerned to think hard about how the new system should be shaped. However, although swift closure enabled an almost complete break with the past, it would have been naive to imagine we were not living in its shadow and influence. A start was being made and there would have to be continuous development as experience was gained in the new setting.

Mission statements and plans were written, but before they could become practical guide-lines we needed field experience, trial and error.

# FOUR GUIDING CONCEPTS

## REMOVE THE HOSPITAL FROM A
## CENTRAL PLACE IN THE CLIENTS' AND
## PROFESSIONALS' LIVES

The first influence was a desire to free clients and staff from the constraints of institutional control, so as to increase their opportunities and choices for personal development. Essentially, this meant removing the hospital from the centre of the clients' and also the professionals' lives. In the heyday of institutionalisation, the community was a place in which people with mental illness or handicap seemed to be 'on probation'. It was as if their natural home was the hospital and they could be away from it only until such time as they failed and had to return. Staff had also been educated to believe that the hospital was the source of professional innovation. Evidence of this attitude came during the inspection of the mental handicap nurse training programme during the early 1980s when one of the visiting inspectors enquired: 'If you get rid of the hospitals how will you train your nurses?' In reply we explained the importance of not programming trainees with ideas which would afterwards have to be unlearned because they were inappropriate. Central to our new philosophy was the idea of maintaining people in the community, which would be the focus for better care and rehabilitation initiatives.

## USING THE HEALTH BUDGET ONLY
## FOR HEALTH ISSUES

The second influence was a radical change in management thinking which came from the discovery that the then orthodox notion of 'big being beautiful and efficient' was mistaken. In a stand alone institution the single budget must cater for everything—the accommodation, the staff and all the treatment and support systems. In the community the health budget is but one of a number of contributing budgets and resources. A simple example is the matter of providing better living accommodation. In the hospital it comes from one single capital allocation, whereas in the community there are council houses, housing associations, voluntary organisations and a host of others all present to provide suitable housing. Friends and enemies regularly warned us of dire consequences once the Government learned how we were cashing in on all these extra benefits for people who were thought to be safely provided for in hospital. They said that reductions would be made to the health budget to compensate for the increase cost in Social Security payments. It always seemed to me that once the patients were in the community and the hospitals closed, any such calculation after the event would be very difficult. In fact, Ministers were well aware of what we were doing and entirely supportive.

## *FASHION PROGRAMMES TO MEET CLIENT NEED*

The third influence was a change in the purpose and methods of assessing clients' needs. Previously, this was a simple process to find the service into which the person could be fitted: e.g. attending a day hospital or occupational therapy department. The new approach was to fashion a specific programme of care and support responsive to the needs of each individual.

## *CONSULTING WITH THE USERS*

The fourth influence was a realisation that the experts did not know best, and that their work would be enhanced through interaction and consultation with clients, interest groups, and communities. One significant development influencing plans for all health services in the Exeter district was the introduction of 'Locality Planning'. Communities were invited to identify themselves and appoint representatives with whom we could work to improve the accessibility and performance of services. These committees of local representatives, professional staff and managers are known as locality planning teams and their work has been very influential in the Exeter district.

Separate services have been set up for people with learning disabilities, the mentally ill, and the confused elderly.

## 1. SERVICES FOR PEOPLE WITH LEARNING DISABILITIES

To ensure that help was close at hand for the 1200 to 1400 clients we expected to serve, six service locations were selected throughout the district, within easy reach of a group of localities. At each community centre we established a team of professional staff, equipped with a local support unit, to work in the community and to be in touch with clients in their own homes. The local support unit has a variety of facilities including a small number of residential places for short term care.

### WHO HELPS?: COMMUNITY TEAMS

Each team comprises a staff (full and part time) of community nurses, social workers, clinical psychologists, doctors, speech, physio and occupational therapists. The team size depends on the number of clients in the localities served.

The community team creates an individual care plan to suit each client's personal needs, and implements it by supporting the individual and family and co-ordinating the activities of all the agencies involved. The intention is to develop the client's skills—so the plan typically includes training to improve self esteem and skills for living. Learning to dry your own hair at 50, going out alone to a cafe for a cup of tea after being locked up for many years, and tending a patch of garden for the first time are the small but humanly significant new experiences this approach has opened up for some.

### WHERE CAN HELP BE FOUND?
### LOCAL SUPPORT UNITS

For each of the six community centres a local support unit offers a 24 hour service and short-term residential care. Each has a few beds to deal with both emergencies and planned respite care to give families and informal carers regular breaks. Services include assessment skill training, and behavioural modification. Clients may attend on a day or residential basis as needs demand. Families and carers can immediately call on the support units in crisis when help for a learning disabled client is needed in a hurry. Formerly, admission to hospital was somehow final, and discharge unlikely. The good thing now is that when the crisis passes it is a small step for the client to return home from the local support unit.

The first unit was purpose built, and took three years to plan and construct. Inevitably, it exceeded the original budget. In hindsight, too many services were grouped on one site—but for the skill and attention of the staff it could easily have become a mini institution. After this experience, we decided to buy and adapt ordinary houses. This has proved a far more appropriate and economic alternative.

### HELP FOR FAMILIES: CHILDREN'S RESPITE CARE

In 1974 one of the first family support units in the world was set up in Exeter. If offered day and respite care for young children. However, one centre in so far flung a district, with families up to 30 miles distant from it, is not enough. It is inconvenient for parents going away for the weekend if considerable extra mileage is incurred to deliver and collect children. So in response to this need three more respite units have been set up in various parts of the district. Though part of the locality services, they offer services to children quite separate from the local support units and usually on a programmed basis rather than in response to emergencies.

### WHERE DO PEOPLE WITH LEARNING DISABILITIES LIVE?: GROUP HOMES AND HOSTELS

Experience in Exeter shows that it is possible for people with learning disabilities, including those with the most profound conditions, to live happily in ordinary houses, provided that there are sufficient staff to help. The majority are in groups of three to six people, but there are two hostels, one of 12 beds and the other seven, which cater for people experiencing their first move from their parental home or hospital before they go on to something smaller.

The most profoundly disabled people, those who are of very low mental ability and who may also be blind, physically disabled, or unable to communicate verbally, some of whom may be subject to bouts of wild behaviour, live in similar houses. The important factor making this possible is a high staffing level, which may be in the order of two or three to one resident. In one of the houses the kitchen has a glazed partition, which in hospital would have been regularly smashed, or replaced by something more substantial for safety reasons. But in their own home the residents treat it with care. The staffing levels are those which are necessary in intensive therapy units in general hospitals. Wherever these disabled people are, they would need the same staffing levels. The fascinating thing is that the staff's job is made easier because the domestic nature of the environment seems to have a calming effect on the residents.

### TRAINING AND EMPLOYMENT OPPORTUNITIES

Before 1980, Exeter was poorly served with day-time activity centres for people with learning disabilities. There were too few, and they offered limited choice to their clients. Consequently, improving them was a high priority when extra funds (Joint Finance) were made available to Social Services and the Health Authority in 1975. The number of towns with a local service has increased from four to eight, and the range of available activities is now wider than before. Tiverton, which had no local service at all, now has several locations, including a shop, 'We've Made It', where you can hire fancy dress and buy items made by the people employed in the small work room at the back. Incidentally, they have presented a hand decorated table cloth to, and much appreciated by, the Maori Nurses Association in New Zealand. When they get fed up with working they can serve in the shop and chat to customers. Day Services in Tiverton also have a contract with British Rail, 'Bloomers', to provide flowers and plants at the new station which serves the area, Tiverton Parkway.

Okehampton, on the edge of Dartmoor particularly resented that its people with learning disabilities had a long journey to their nearest training centre, so a house was bought (by the Health Authority) in the town, large enough to serve a number of purposes including provision of day-time activities. Its informal atmosphere ensures that it is not simply the preserve of professional staff but that everyone can share in the activities there.

### CONSULTATION AND WATCH-DOG:
### LOCAL PLANNING TEAMS

Guiding the development of each local service is a planning team, comprised of parents and professional representatives from education, social services and health. Three teams now also have a client member. The teams are just one of the measures introduced to ensure that services do respond to needs, rather than people fitting into services. They have been particularly effective in shaping the new day services and extending integration into the community wherever possible. In Okehampton disabled people have been welcomed as full members of the local youth club. At Axminster a hobbies club has been set up so that disabled people can be introduced to various activities such as stamp collecting, model building, outdoor activities, and a host of other things, and not by paid professionals, but by local enthusiasts.

## 2. COMMUNITY MENTAL HEALTH SERVICES

One great advantage of community mental health services is the absence of the stigma which attached to attending a mental hospital. Because clients are seen informally, often in their own homes, they feel more at ease and willing to take advantage of the services. A much wider range of help and support for clients and their families can be offered than was possible when everything was hospital based. However, there is still a hospital element to the work and it would be wrong to suggest that this has disappeared entirely, or that it is never needed.

### COMMUNITY MENTAL HEALTH TEAMS AND MENTAL HEALTH CENTRES

Mental Health Centre is rather a grand title for the ordinary houses in which mental health teams are based. They are located for ease of client access. So long as they provide all that is needed in the way of offices and small meeting rooms, it is important that they are indistinguishable from the rest of the buildings on the street.

Five teams are spread across the district, each comprising community psychiatric nurses, one or two consultant psychiarists, a clinical psychologist, an occupational-therapist, social workers and a Centre secretary. The number in each team depends on the size of the client population in the localities served.

When the teams were first set up, every client was referred to the consultant psychiatrist. But this point of access now accounts for less than 20 per cent of the case load, and access to individual team members has been extended considerably. The majority of referrals are by family doctors to the consultant, to individual team members, or simply to the team. Self-referral is another option. Clients can walk in off the street and ask for help. At weekly team meetings, new referrals are reviewed, to ensure that each has a key team member who is known both to the person and to his or her family doctor. Much care and thought has been given to ensure that the system works and is understood and accepted by the other health and community agencies.

The types of cases are wide ranging and include people with acute mental health problems and those with long term mental health disabilities. The work is with individuals, families and groups and is as much to do with assisting people to cope with day to day practical problems—such as getting the correct Social Security benefits and understanding the Community Charge—as specific drug therapies and stress management programmes. Hospital admission, for those clients who cannot be managed in the community, is available at the new Cedars unit and at Wonford House hospital—both situated on the site of the District General Hospital in Exeter.

### FOR PEOPLE WITH LONG TERM PSYCHIATRIC PROBLEMS: REHABILITATION SERVICES

Because of a build up over the years of people discharged from the mental hospitals and congregated in Exeter, we decided a group of professional staff was needed for them, in addition to the community teams. In many ways, the requirements of this group, with long term mental health problems, are similar to those of people with learning disabilities. They need full social support to cater for accommodation, work, leisure and social opportunities. Among them are many who experience the greatest difficulty in assimilating into society and for whom special opportunities are valuable. 'Spring Board' is one such enterprise which finds useful activity for a number of quite disabled people— by decorating houses, and tending gardens for example, they have shown that they have a useful contribution to make. The supportive relationship of working together as a group is essential for them. There are also social clubs or drop in centres where people know they will find familiar and friendly faces.

Group homes and hostels have been established which cater for their needs. The rehabilitation services also have special hostels for the times when some people are in need of close and attentive care. But, unlike in the days of the old locked wards of the hospital, they resume their ordinary lives when the crisis passes.

## 3. SERVICES FOR ELDERLY
## CONFUSED PEOPLE

Exeter was one of the first places, in the early 1970s, to set up a joint psycho-geriatric and geriatric assessment service to ensure that elderly confused people were not all immediately assumed to have Alzheimer's Disease. Care was taken to see whether their disorientation was attributable to a vitamin deficiency, heart condition, or any other reason which was capable of treatment and improvement. However, once they were diagnosed as having an irreversible condition, they were transferred to the long-stay wards. There they and their families found an atmosphere of hopelessness which communicated itself to residents and staff alike.

Replacing the central hospital are nine local services, with beds for short-term care, day-centres, and domiciliary teams whose job it is to see that people get a network of care from all the social agencies properly co-ordinated and meeting the need at the time required. Very often a confused elderly person has only an elderly spouse to care for them. The assistance of a key team member, a known local person, to interpret needs and co-ordinate services is invaluable to avoid the home help, bath attendant and community nurse all turning up on the doorstep at once—or long periods without any help at all.

The domiciliary services have found the value of not spending all their money on staff and other running costs, but keeping some as reserve. 'A bag of money', as these funds are called, means that services or equipment can be brought for individuals to suit their individual requirements and assist them to stay at home for as long as possible.

When nursing home care is called for, this is provided mainly by private nursing homes. State funds are available to them only for this style of care, whereas the Health Authority can use its resources for domiciliary support. Thereby each team will typically be supporting 160 confused elderly people in the community.

The Health Authority's Homes for the Elderly Confused provide respite care for families who care for their elderly relative at home, and who do not want their partner or parent to go into permanent care in a nursing home, and yet who appreciate a break from round the clock care. The service also sponsors support groups for the carers and this is of inestimable help to wives and husbands, giving the chance to chat over problems with people who help them to understand the problems they experience.

The Homes for the Elderly Confused have all been designed to make the environment and style more domestic than clinical. There is now some evidence that the despair and hopelessness which many experienced formerly has been overcome, both because of this and because the families and friends can more easily remain in contact with an elderly relative.

These services are important for a district in which 19 per cent of the population are elderly and with increasing numbers aged over 80.


## CONCLUSION

This chapter offers a thumbnail sketch of the range of services which have replaced the mental hospitals in Exeter. They do not satisfy all demands. As services improve so the public's expectations rise, bringing new reasons for disappointment with what is on offer. However, there is clear approval for them being local, accessible, small scale, ordinary and informal—the help comes without the old stigma. People with mental health problems and learning disabilities regard it as important that they can still make decisions and have a say in their care. Not being called patients is important to them. These high ideals are not always attained, but they are in the philosophy of community services and so there is a constant drive to see that professional practice pays attention to them.

# 6

# The management of change: people in the NHS

## NETWORK OF CO-OPERATION IS THE KEY TO SUCCESS

Turning now to the forces which brought about the changes, I make no excuse for starting with the contribution of the people involved, both from within and outside the NHS. Management methods and money have played their part but the most significant factor has been the commitment, enthusiasm, imagination, hard work, and resourcefulness of hundreds of people. That is hard fact, not a trite compliment. When people are convinced that a thing is right, and are consulted, listened to, and treated fairly, no change is too great and the result is built on firm foundations.

A network of co-operation and support has been fashioned which includes patients, their families and representative organisations, the staff, trade unions, authority members, local authority and voluntary agencies, councillors, members of parliament and the public. This network is not a dewy-eyed optional extra, but rather the keystone of success, for we were often told that there were elements in the community keen to oppose the changes if only a bandwagon of protest had started to roll.

## PATIENTS, THEIR FAMILIES AND SUPPORTERS FAVOUR NEW COMMUNITY SERVICES

Consumer satisfaction and support for the community services, and the total lack of nostalgia for hospital life, was recorded in Chapter 2. Apparently derelict lives have found new meaning and purpose. People silent for years have, after a short time of the new life, spoken and gone out to buy the daily papers. Families and carers formerly conditioned to lonely and dedicated lives of constant duty have discovered fellowship, support, advice, and practical help. So far as the customers are concerned the programme has been successful.

## PSYCHIATRISTS ARE OFTEN OPPOSED TO HOSPITAL CLOSURE

In some parts of the country psychiatrists have actively opposed community policies. But this has not happened in Exeter, and without their support much less would have been possible. The consultant psychiatrists were the joint authors and leaders of change in mental handicap care in partnership with nurses, psychologists and administrators/managers.

In the mental health area it was one of the psychiatrists at Exminster who inspired the changes. Though that movement could have been led by the doctors, as a body they never generated the necessary support and conviction. Despite this, the importance of staying in touch with medical opinion was clearly recognised, and throughout the period of change the task of the Chairman of the Consultants' Committee has been of key significance. It was not an easy job to explain the changes to colleagues, and to ensure that management decisions were shown to be influenced by their advice. We were fortunate that the Chairman who was in office for much of the time managed to maintain the delicate balance which gave sufficient sanction for action and avoided outright opposition.

The Royal College of Psychiatrists is not enthusiastically in favour of the demise of the mental hospitals. In 1986 at a College meeting held in Torbay the matter was debated. The Chairman of the Exeter psychiatrists spoke in favour of the changes, but the vote at the end was overwhelmingly against care in the community.

One reason for this must be that for many years the authority of the doctors has been under challenge from the other mental health professions. In hospitals doctors still have the basic responsibilities for admission, discharge, and the prescription of treatment, whereas community care gives greater scope for independent action by the other professions. Interprofessional politics is a strong element in determining attitudes to the two models of care. It has to be said also that there is a degree of rivalry among the other professions, which strengthens the argument for 'generic' mental health workers.

But this is not the whole story. Throughout the 1960s and 1970s, psychiatrists have seen a building programme to modernise district general hospitals, and investment in so called 'high tech' medicine—heart transplants, body scanners, and the like. Yet for mental health there has been no comparable investment of interest and money. Psychiatrists have a real concern that there is no commitment, and merely a wish to sweep the problems under the carpet. For this reason they feel obliged to oppose hospital closure.

## NURSES GAIN NEW OPPORTUNITIES AND ACCEPT HOSPITAL CLOSURES

If the doctors have most to lose, it is the nurses who have most to gain from community care, for it increases their scope of professional activity and offers far more individual responsibility than the traditional nursing roles in the mental hospitals afford. For them the change has been little short of the rebirth of a profession. There have always been dedicated and good nurses in mental hospitals, but often the nursing staff seemed the most resistant to change and improvement, and willing to support colleagues whose standards were not of the highest order.

In the over-crowded wards there was little incentive or opportunity for nurses to respond to the needs of individual patients. Hospital routines kept many charge nurses involved in continuous administrative activity and away from their patients. The psychiatric nurses were active trade unionists and COHSE, their main trade union, had a reputation for militancy. There had been a nursing strike at Digby Hospital in 1972. Threats of work to rule, press statements critical of management, votes of no confidence in managers, were all methods of intimidation employed in a war with management which smouldered over the years.

Against this background it was remarkable that some wards were havens of homely security and worthwhile activity. What immense qualities of leadership their charge nurses possessed to overcome all the inhumanity of the institutional system, for it was this and not the nurses who were really at fault. The mental hospital system produced poor behaviour among the staff as well as the patients. What chance did they stand when for much of the time there were only two nurses to look after wards of 20 and 30 demanding patients? The system did not encourage initiative, indeed worked in a variety of ways to thwart it, and was quick to criticise and punish the smallest variations from the rules.

I have witnessed many occasions when the invisible dead hand of the institution crushed personal initiative. In one hospital the desire to provide more normal clothing resulted in the issue of jackets normal in every respect save that they opened at the back to stop the patients playing with the zip. In 1987, I witnessed a battle royal which raged all one morning between ward staff and clerks in the hospital office who refused to make a cash allowance for a patient to go to the hairdressers because too little notice had been given. The hospital system always seems to be against anyone showing a spark of initiative. At first the news of hospital closure was received with disbelief and scorn: the nursing staff had heard it all before. When the first ward closed at Starcross Hospital and was demolished, the patch of grass which replaced it was so small that the gap was hardly noticed. It was very far from being the dramatic signal for change we had intended. But the programme rolled on and gradually the message was communicated.

Once freed from the institutional constraints, the nursing staff have shown themselves able to respond to the greater initiative and responsibility open to them in the new-style services. In Exeter the former hospital nursing staff have created the new community services. The process has been a cascade. It started with a few nurses accepting the challenge, and their success gave confidence to ever increasing numbers who saw that far from being a sell out, it was a golden opportunity for better care for the people they served.

## OTHER PROFESSIONAL GROUPS: SOCIAL WORKERS, OCCUPATIONAL THERAPISTS, AND CLINICAL PSYCHOLOGISTS, AT HOME IN THE COMMUNITY

The community is the natural working environment for social workers, so the change presented them with no major problems. Hospital occupational therapists were quick to seize the new opportunities offered by systems of community care. One good example of this is arranging for former hospital patients to assist in the restoration of small craft at Exeter's Maritime Museum, 'therapy' with purpose and meaning.

Modern clinical psychology has been of major importance in introducing an appropriate style for community care, one which encourages people to discover their own resourcefulness to overcome problems. The Health Authority's clinical psychology department and the post-graduate training course it runs in conjunction with Exeter University Psychology Department date from 1975. The Department has therefore grown up with the new community services, and has a thorough commitment to and experience of the community approach. This well deserved reputation has always ensured a flow of good postgraduate trainees. My recollections of their contribution over the years include the introduction to us of the new status of patients as equals, and a willingness to share skills and train other staff in a multi-disciplinary setting.

A clinical psychologist has led an evaluation team whose approach, founded in the theory and practice of 'Normalisation', has been both innovative and effective in helping staff to shape services to meet the needs of their clients. A list of the Evaluation Team's reports is in the Appendix at the end of the book.

## TRADE UNIONS SUPPORT THE CHANGE

Trade Unions have supported all the changes and helped to make them work. Adopting this positive stance has been a harder role for them than the traditional one of being in permanent opposition to management. Some of their members have been deeply distrustful of what they see as an unnatural collusion between unions and management.

Perhaps the Unions had become as dissatisfied as management with the tedious round of negotiation to improve the hospitals. How often over the years we had gathered in the Board Room at Exminster for lengthy discussions—for example, to negotiate alterations to the shift systems so that nurses no longer worked 12 hours at a stretch, or to get the last meal of the day for patients served later than 4.30 in the afternoon. The joint meeting of management with the trade unions was usually preceded by each side meeting separately to prepare its ground and anticipate what the other might have in store.

Gradually, we learned that far from having different aims we shared a common purpose and progress was made. There was, however, an element of competition as to whether it was the unions or management inspiring the changes. The tone and style of formal meetings differed little from in the old days, but in small working parties the traditional aggressive tones were abandoned and effective joint co-operation took place. There was considerable constructive endeavour, achieved with representatives on the staff who were members of

COHSE, NALGO, NUPE, GMWU, and other organisations usually thought to be resistant to change. In Exeter they were far sighted, reasonable, courageous, and sensible: all the qualities they are usually accused of lacking. They were very ably led by a chairman and a secretary, who in turn were supported by a well informed committee in contact with grass root opinion, ensuring they did not lose touch with what was acceptable to their members, and therefore, possible. It was an enormous benefit that all the negotiations were conducted by our own staff and not by paid union officials, simply because this shortened lines of communication.

Negotiations were helped by a national initiative within COHSE which looked ahead to the demise of the big hospitals and the dawn of comprehensive community policies. This had been led by a national officer of the union, the late Terry Mallinson, whose untimely death before the report was complete was a great loss. The Secretary of the largest COHSE branch in Exeter was a member of this committee and brought the benefits of national thinking to the local level.

Criticisms have sometimes been voiced that too much time was devoted to trade union negotiation, instead of telling the staff what management intended to do. At the time we commenced these changes in the early 1980s such a policy was simply not possible—even had it been desirable—for it was long before the power of trade unions had been challenged. More importantly, without thorough discussion we would not have developed such an effective and comprehensive range of services, with staff so committed to their success, nor would the work have been able to benefit from the vast experience the staff have to offer.


## EXETER HEALTH AUTHORITY

In so political an arena as mental health there have been many aspects of the work which could be done only by members of the Health Authority. Their support for the policies has been consistent, but the need has been for more than passive loyalty. There has been work for them too. They have shouldered the press criticisms, encouraged the staff and interpreted the process to their local communities. They have assisted in negotiating community solutions with local government agencies. For example, one member of the Health Authority, who was also an elected councillor, successfully fought the opposition from members of her own political party in a District Council to the acquisition by the Health Authority of a plot of ground for a local unit to serve the elderly confused people.

A key feature of the hospital closure programme was that the Health Authority would establish and manage accommodation in the community for some hospital patients. The first hostel for former long-term patients at Exminster was set up in 1983. At this and the other hostels and group homes the residents paid rent out of their Social Security benefits. It was a funding mechanism which had the full support of Ministers and senior officials of the combined Department of Health and Social Security in London. Then, with little warning, at Christmastime 1986, the procedure was declared by the Department to be an unauthorised use of funds, and to cease forthwith. But there was no guidance how the accommodation was to be funded. Members of the Authority readily joined with managers to find an answer.

The objection to the scheme had been that it was run by the Health Authority. The solution adopted was the creation of a charitable trust to take over responsibility for providing the homes and hostels. This new venture, Home Care Trust, now has 16 hostels and homes of various kinds, with places for over 200 people. The trust leases the properties from the Health Authority which also provides extra funding above the residents' welfare benefits to achieve the required staffing levels. The Trust's directors were insistent that their responsibilities extended beyond the ordinary remit of a health authority to ensure that former hospital residents were appropriately catered for in the community. Home Care

Trust is tangible evidence of the Health Authority's interest in and commitment to the programmes of reform.

Small groups of Health Authority members were deputed to take a close interest in the various services, to contribute to policy and monitor progress. This work has kept them fully informed and able to contribute to policy as it is being shaped. The support of a well informed group of Health Authority members has assisted staff in their work and reinforced their confidence.

Political friendships have been put at risk, and many a happy party evening spoiled as members have remained faithful to a cause about which many of their friends outside the Health Authority had serious doubts.

## THE DEPARTMENT OF HEALTH AND THE REGIONAL HEALTH AUTHORITY

In the absence of a comprehensive national policy on care in the community, the record shows the willingness of ministers and officials at the Department of Health and Social Security to support local action and initiative. There were two occasions when this support was invaluable. The first was the speedy assistance to get Home Care Trust the support it needed to become established. The second was in excusing Exeter from a national time-table for competitive tendering of domestic and catering services. This programme, begun in 1985, challenged the cost of directly employed services with those provided by private contractors. It was highly controversial and opposed by the trade unions. As it coincided with a time of critical change for the psychiatric services when union co-operation was essential, the damage could have been considerable. So intent was the government on the programme that to be excused from it required ministerial approval. Exeter was the only Authority in England for whom a delay in implementation was agreed.

Likewise, the Regional Health Authority supported the Health Authority's endeavours, only differing on the topic of services for people with mental handicap which it believed should have been handed over to Social Services. Perhaps the most valuable contribution afforded by the Regional Authority and the Department has been to encourage Exeter to get on and solve its own problems.

## REWARDS AND INCENTIVES

What has motivated this broad range of co-operation? The changes we set out to make were more political than managerial. They could not have been achieved by simply relying on managerial authority to force things through. Success depended crucially on establishing a broad consensus of approval. Failure to get the politics right could have resulted in an orchestrated opposition of worried staff and families who would have found little difficulty in overturning the Health Authority's plans. By listening to various interest groups and responding to their anxieties we avoided this in Exeter. If it sounds too good to be true, please do not underestimate the enormous investment made in effective consultation— listening, explaining, adjusting. The process of listening made us aware of the staff and public's major concerns which would have to be dealt with if we were able to gain their support. For the staff, hospital closure was synonymous with loss of livelihood. They needed the assurance that if they agreed to change, their careers would not be at risk. This was given by the Health Authority, and as the community services developed it became clear that career prospects were better than in the hospital system with its ever present prospect of closure. Community care offers assured future employment for the staff and more fulfilling professional activity. This is a factor which is now amply proved in the number and range of job opportunities. Closure of hospitals has not meant cuts in service but more job opportunities. Offering the hospital staff the guarantee of a place in the new services was an essential plank to win their support. But is it needed — there is no shortage of people to fill the po...

The great fear for the community was to have what many perceived as the 'mad' and 'bad' living next door instead of in a hospital a long way off. The re-assurance was that there would be locally based staff on hand to help to provide more and better local health services. This was treated with suspicion among rural communities used to the withdrawal of all kinds of services, always with the unfulfilled promise of something more effective to replace them. For example, when local railway services were closed it was on the understanding that good bus services would be introduced. Too often the reality had fallen far short of the promise. The difference was that on this occasion a health authority was offering to close something central so as to open more, and better local services. Understandably, the offer of more local services in the communities of east and mid Devon was so unexpected that it was regarded with suspicion. But as the new units and additional community staff have spread out, the change has been welcomed. Not only has this meant greater local presence and therefore access, but also the opportunity for more involvement by local people in managing these services. The customers now have more influence on the way things are done.

With the staff and local communities on our side, the new services could move forward with confidence. Indeed, all parties to the changes have found an enthusiasm flowing from the challenge of doing something first and against the trend.

All these things aside, the great joy of the National Health Service is that it employs people who are interested in doing their best for others. Perhaps that is why the British are so deeply distrustful of anyone performing these services for personal profit. Consequently, the main incentive motivating all who are involved has undoubtedly been the greater benefits which the new services have brought to those who use them. They are more consumer orientated and acceptable than the old mental hospitals. Which is not to suggest that if you float above Devon you will hear only a purr of satisfaction from the ground. That would be expecting the impossible. But, I believe, there is nobody who wants the clock turned back.

—> that's ok when you have a job in the new service.

# 7

# Community relations: myths and realities

## A CARING COMMUNITY?
## PARTICIPATION IN THE CHANGE
## IS ESSENTIAL

One telling criticism of the policy of Care in the Community is the ample evidence that the 'community' couldn't care less about the plight of the mentally afflicted and is hostile to their interests. Therefore, runs the argument, until the 'community' shows greater concern there is good reason to protect the vulnerable from it and maintain the shelter of mental hospitals.

But the community can only learn to care if it participates in change and has a part in providing alternatives. This means explaining, consulting and sharing responsibility.

Lip service is given to participation and consultation, but real commitment to involve the community as equals in decision-making is often lacking. People are not stupid, and they can tell the difference between sham and authentic participation. Community involvement complicates the process and it takes time for people who have previously been excluded from decision making to gain confidence that the offer is genuine. This comes only when they see results flowing from participation. The experience in Devon and Exeter has been gloomy at times, but the overall picture is of a growing acceptance and positive community response.

## THE DOWNSIDE: PLANNING PERMISSION
## FREQUENTLY OBSTRUCTED

Anyone listening to the objections of prospective neighbours to a proposed group home or hostel would conclude that the community is not awash with the milk of human kindness. Because of this predictable negative response authorities in some parts of the country have simply gone ahead without consulting neighbours. But we were attempting such large transfers of people from the institutions to ordinary housing that consultation seemed the only sensible thing to do. It was the way to recruit the support of local politicians who were best placed to explain the ideas to their electorate. And so, in addition to submitting planning applications and attending local authority planning committee meetings, we also met prospective neighbours to tell them our intentions whenever a group home or hostel was under consideration. There have been scores of these meetings, all of them calling for tact and diplomacy. With a few rare and blessed exceptions they have been opportunities for an endless parade of all the customary concerns and prejudices: fears of physical violence and sexual impropriety, laced with an underlying concern about diminishing property values.

The choice was whether to run a series of general public meetings to explain our intentions, or to tackle each housing project separately. We chose the latter to avoid arousing general public alarm and opposition from people who might never be affected. A few journalists considered this conspiratorial, and pressed us to declare the whole hand, but we managed to keep them at bay.

The press was not sympathetic, and consistently publicised and supported the objections to our plans and at times had a field day. Exeter's evening paper seemed to be the most willing to print scare stories of what might befall the neighbours of discharged patients. Sadly, the more educated and middle class the group affected, the more prominent and lurid the story. Sometimes the opposition was so aggressive that we decided not to proceed with a house purchase: but this happened on only a few occasions. In the majority of instances the objectors have since learned that their fears were unfounded. When neighbours subsequently apologised for their initial hostility the papers have not reported it. There is no legal protection against the expression and publication of this form of prejudice. It would be a marvellous step if the press and media exercised self-imposed restraint.

Public involvement in the business of house purchase and planning approval showed the community at its least compassionate. Nevertheless, the hostels and group homes have been set up, and after a time the new neighbours have settled down well together. Happily, there have been other, more encouraging, facets of community involvement and these are described in the rest of this chapter.

## JOINT CONSULTATIVE COMMITTEES (JCC) WITH COUNTY COUNCIL AND DISTRICT COUNCILS

JCCs were introduced in the mid 1970s to encourage effective co-ordination among agencies which together provide all the social services: education, housing, employment, health care, and social services. It is a government requirement that all the statutory and voluntary agencies should meet together with the purpose of weaving their services into a seamless garment to serve those in need. The fuel for this co-operation is a fund of money known as Joint Finance allocated to health authorities but to be spent by mutual agreement with local councils. It is a pump priming fund, which means that the money is available to individual projects for a few years after which local authorities must find the permanent operating costs for them. Then the original money becomes available again for new projects and the cycle continues. In theory, one allocation of Joint Finance can, over a period of years, generate several times its value of local authority expenditure.

Local government complained that this left health authorities with the bun and the penny, and allowing them to introduce new priorities for money local government authorities intended for other purposes. This has been the cause of deep resentment and accounts for a general view that JCCs have been a failure.

Happily, there has been no lack of co-operation in Devon where the various authorities have made it work. The time-table has been driven by hospital closure, and an awareness that this release of resources has enabled the development of services and resources to all parts of the county. The major funding has come from the hospitals, and Joint Finance has been the icing on the cake. Because the resources were available, plans could be implemented, and communities could see the build up of services locally, just as the programme promised.

There have been two distinct phases of joint consultation as the nature of the work changed. In the first half of the 1980s the emphasis was on the Devon JCC to measure the impact of the hospital decentralisation, the dispersal of patients, and division of funds among the four health authorities and the County Social Services Department. When the hospitals had closed, the need for and value of joint consultation was a local matter and the four District JCCs grew in importance.

## THE DEVON COUNTY JOINT
## CONSULTATIVE COMMITTEE

This comprised County Council representatives, elected members and officers from the Education, Social Services, Treasurer's and Chief Executive's Departments. There were also members and managers from the four Health Authorities and three representatives of voluntary societies. The ten District Councils also wished to be members, but no satisfactory method of representation could be worked out such that the already large committee would not grow to unworkable proportions.

The County JCC had much work to do between 1982 and 1986. The closure of the mental health and mental handicap hospitals in Exeter resulted in the transfer of former patients and associated resources to the Torbay,

Plymouth, and North Devon Health Authorities. Each Health Authority had a different approach, though they would all be working with the one County Social Services Department.

The flexible and accommodating response of Social Services to these varied policies owes much to the enlightened attitude and spirit of co-operation of the two succeeding County Directors during the period. It would have been so easy to have insisted on a uniform policy, but administrative considerations were set aside to facilitate progress. The Social Services Department itself became convinced of the benefits of decentralisation, was reorganised in 1987/88, and its local management is now based in the communities served, whose boundaries match these of the health authority localities.

Despite difficult financial times, the County has allocated money for the permanent funding of joint finance projects. The County Treasurer and his four health authority colleagues have interpreted the arcane financial regulations so that they work to Devon's advantage. None of this happened by magic and initially there were some very hard negotiations. But the authorities did not walk away from each other, and kept talking until a sensible bargain was struck.

### DISTRICT JOINT CONSULTATIVE COMMITTEES

The increasing decentralisation of services to each of Devon's four Health Authority Districts gradually altered the focus for joint consultation. The sensible conclusion was to sub-divide the county JCC and concentrate the work in four district JCCs. The key county departments, Social Services, and Education have seats on each district JCC and work with the local Health Authority, District Councils and voluntary agencies.

The boundaries of the district councils do not coincide with those of the County Council areas and health authorities' districts. Devon is not alone in this lack of co-terminosity. It is an administrative complexity repeated nation-wide and is often considered to be a hindrance to effective joint action. In the part of east Devon served by the Exeter Health Authority there are no fewer than five District Councils, but far from being an administrative nightmare it is a real boon. Suppose there was only one unhelpful district council: that would be a genuine obstacle. Instead, all five are progressive—each in its own way—and the occasionally tardy can be spurred on by the achievements of the swifter. Suppose, again, that there were only one helpful district council: it would have one priority list. In east Devon there are five, each independent of the others and with its own top priority—five things to be done first, instead of one.

At the outset there was resistance from some local councils to the allocation of council houses for former hospital residents. They already had long waiting lists and little enthusiasm for another source of demand. Nevertheless they did make some houses available. As we did business together it became apparent there was land owned by the Health Authority which would, if released by hospital closure, be of interest to local councils planning to build new housing estates and such projects have materialised.

Local councils became aware that this was not simply an opportunist, 'flavour of the month' policy, and have become as fully committed to its success as the Health Authority. As in all aspects of our relationships with outside agencies, it has taken time for the key people, members and officials, to get to know and trust each other, and to build the goodwill essential for effective joint co-operation.

The Planning Committees have been universally helpful and guided us through the processes which assist formal applications to be successful. What this means is informal consultation at a very local level so that the statutory application then becomes a formality.

## COMMUNITY HEALTH COUNCIL (CHC): A PUBLIC WATCH-DOG SUPPORTING COMMUNITY CARE

CHCs were established in 1975 as public watch-dogs over the activities of health authorities. There is an obligation for health authorities to consult them on service changes. In Exeter the relationship between the Health Authority and the CHC has always been close and effective. The CHC has genuinely represented the public interest. In the mid 1970s it was very critical of mental hospital conditions and strongly argued for their replacement by community services. There has been no deviation from this policy and it remains a keen advocate and champion of the community services. Indeed, at times their complaint has been the lack of speedier progress. The CHC was closely involved in planning and commenting on the changes and has never flinched from defending them in the teeth of critical comment.

One useful contribution made by the CHC has been that many of its members have since become members of the Health Authority. The Authority's Chairman previously chaired the CHC. The continuity has been of great value because the new members were already briefed and committed to what was being done.

## VOLUNTARY ORGANISATIONS: IN TUNE WITH CONSUMER NEEDS

There is a bewildering array of local and national voluntary organisations and many of them have contributed significantly to the various programmes. Theirs is an important voice because of the trend for consumers to participate in the management of community services. Voluntary organisations better reflect the needs and wishes of the consumer than the statutory authorities on which consumer representation is perhaps less influential.

## LOCALITY PLANNING TEAMS AND LOCAL PLANNING TEAMS: COMMUNITY INVOLVEMENT IN PLANNING

The Exeter district has been divided into more than 20 natural communities or localities and within each a Locality Planning Team has been formed. The teams include staff working for health, social services, and education within the locality, as well as the police, churches, voluntary organisations, and local councillors.

The purpose of the Teams is to better understand the needs of small communities and to improve service co-operation at the grass roots. Staff from the decentralising mental health and learning disability services have become members of these Teams, and this has fostered considerable understanding among local organisations about what the new services have to offer and how to access them. In return, local communities have taken opportunities to provide support for the new services. Working together has assisted the process of integration. For example, the members of one Locality Planning Team saw the new inhabitants of a group home as people with a need to make social contact in their new surroundings, and set about, of their own accord, to help. Tony Day has written an account of locality planning in the Exeter Health District, published by Bristol University entitled *Getting Closer to the Consumer?* (see Appendix 1).

To ensure that people with learning disabilities and their families get the local service they need Local Planning Teams have been set up which give service users the opportunity to influence the way things are organised and managed. Six Local Planning Teams serve the Exeter District, whose membership comprises health and social services staff (nurses, social workers, psychologists, and doctors), parents, and local representatives of Mencap, the voluntary organisation representing the needs of people with learning disabilities. Membership has now been extended to include people with learning disabilities, and though it took a little while to establish their claim to a voice, this is now well accepted. Each team responds to the needs of individuals and families in the locality it serves.

## MEMBERS OF PARLIAMENT: VITAL ALLIES

Throughout the programme of change, the Devon Members of Parliament have been informed of developments. Briefing them has its advantages for they are often the first port of call for protesters whose objections can effectively be nipped in the bud by an MP who knows that a public authority is behaving responsibly and will listen and modify its plans.

*                    *                    *

Trying to impose the reorganisation of psychiatric services on the community simply because it is the right thing to do would have failed in Devon. But working with the community has paid rich dividends and enabled the realisation of our plans. The formal network has been important but is only a crude grid which enables individuals to work effectively. No administrative structure, however complex and well intentioned, is the real key to success. As in all local communities, there are some leading people who wear several hats and are active in a variety of spheres. It is the network of personal relationships among people who want to get something done which produces results.

# 8

# The management of change

In management circles there is no more popular topic than 'the management of change', and the principles are well known. There must be an acceptance that change is needed, effective agents to lead it, methods of controlling and measuring progress, and a culture that gives confidence to the organisation so that change is an orderly process.

What science there is to inform us about the management of change stops short at distinguishing between the significance of different change projects. There seems to be no accepted way of determining the depth and breadth of change. The usual measures of scale, the total financial value or the numbers of staff affected, are not in themselves sufficient for this purpose. Other factors have to be taken into account measuring such things as whether the purpose of the business has changed, the degree of difference between the old and new working practices, the level of input by the people involved in designing the new, and whether it is a novel change or one for which there is precedent and models to follow. A 'Richter Scale' of change is needed so that all these dimensions could be taken into account.

Exeter offers a comparison to illustrate the point. Fifteen years ago we commissioned a brand new District General Hospital of 400 beds, the Royal Devon and Exeter. Since then it has developed a condition popularly called 'concrete cancer'. The building fabric and foundations are cracking up, and in a few short years it will no longer be safe for people to occupy. Though its

73

grey concrete slab ward tower little graced the Exeter skyline, the hospital has been very successful. Doctors, nurses, and patients like the place and will be sad to see it go: but it must be replaced.

In record time—thanks to the time-table set by 'concrete cancer' and the hard work of many—the new hospital is rising from the ground, a £56m project which will be the workplace for nearly 2000 people treating many thousands of patients each year. The new hospital will be more than a replacement of the present structure. It incorporates many new ideas, will enable services on three separate sites to be brought together on one, and will be more efficient and cost effective to manage. This has been change on a big scale, measured in resources and managerial effort. Compare this with the changes in mental health and mental handicap. The people working in Exeter's mental hospitals became convinced that to give better service to their customers they must leave behind the old asylums. They were given the opportunity to make the transformation using their imagination, experience, and hard work. They chose to make the change themselves. It was not a task imposed from outside. There were no specific allocations of money from the government, only the resources used to run the hospital services and existing community funds such as housing moneys and Social Security benefits which we had never previously tapped. The changes are consumer orientated—aimed at giving people the style of services they want to meet their needs—in place of a service which suppressed the individual.

These two projects have important differences. The new hospital will be a replacement of something which already exists: there are patterns to follow both in the construction and the style of working. It can draw on the extensive experience of a national hospital building programme which has been running since the mid 1960s. By comparison, there have been few precedents to follow in what has been attempted in mental health and mental handicap. We were not simply replacing, but breaking the old mould and fashioning something new for which there were few patterns to follow and no management experience to guide us. Every aspect of it has been novel. That is the crucial difference.

Both are important and large scale projects, measured in terms of money and workforce, but they differ fundamentally in the depth and magnitude of change. When building new hospitals there is a well worn path to follow. Until there are similar patterns and methods to guide managers changing psychiatric services, such projects will continue to be far more demanding.

With the benefit of hindsight, we can describe a number of key elements in the change process. We were not always aware of them at the time, however, because we were having to work instinctively, by trial and error.

## KEY ELEMENTS IN THE CHANGE PROCESS FROM OUR EXPERIENCE

### ACCEPTING THE NEED FOR CHANGE IS THE ESSENTIAL BEGINNING

*See Article (4) Employ usr closing as example of highlighting the need to change*

Organisations are subject to the same laws of survival as animal life—adapt and thrive; ignore change and perish. The job of top management is to sense in what direction change will occur and to provide every incentive and spur for the organisation and its staff to adapt with enthusiasm.

Oddly enough, the business of organisational change has similarities with clinical practice. All the techniques health professionals use to change their clients' behaviour are similar to those employed to bring about organisational change. In theory, the experience and knowledge the staff of the mental hospitals gained from their clinical practice could have been applied to cure the hospitals' ills. They might have recognised in themselves features with which they are well acquainted when dealing with individual clients.

But the block was at the first step. The first necessary

condition for improvement to commence is acceptance of the need for change, and this may take time to develop.

People with a health problem often know it is there, but do not want to recognise it, and try to keep it to themselves. This is like the situation in the mental hospitals at the beginning of the 1970s when the Exeter District Management Team was instructed to keep away, and leave things alone. There were clear signs of an inability for self cure. The mental hospitals spawned working parties and committees endlessly meeting and reporting—but nothing happened. Money and extra resources were given to the hospitals, but there was no light at the end of the tunnel. More problems crowded in to replace any solved. For many people this kind of activity is enough. They might be described as 'organisational hypochondriacs', people who relish talking about their aches and pains and do nothing to remedy them.

The next step for many patients is to see a doctor, but without any commitment to alter a life-style which contributes to their health problem. Having failed themselves, they call upon the expert, but still with the unconscious intention of proving that nothing can be done. So it was with the mental hospitals. After keeping their distance from the Exeter District Management Team, they then requested its involvement, but without any acceptance that new solutions were necessary.

The forces of the status quo were very strong and had proved themselves effective. What several of us considered to be healthy seeds of improvement were not acceptable to those unwilling to give up the old ways. Fortunately, some did take a more constructive view, and we worked with them. Our shared motivation was quite straightforward: a concern for the patients who got such a raw deal in hospital; a desire to assist those staff who were successfully experimenting with community solutions; a conviction that more services could be decentralised; and a preference for the radical alternative.

At the beginning there were a few sparks of change: the problem was how to fan them into a consuming fire. It was a matter of playing every card available to convince the leading professional staff that change was inevitable. Re-organisation working parties were formed and plied with information which showed the way forward. We took parties to other places where new styles of work were being attempted, and organised study days and conferences out of the hospitals to give people the chance to talk and think, away from the stultifying thrall of the big institutions. Much time and effort was devoted to the collection and presentation of real information about the hospitals in Exeter and what was happening. Though little seemed to be changing on the surface, the facts were that the mental handicap hospitals were slowly emptying and the mental hospitals were filling up with confused elderly people. The old order was changing, but the mental hospitals were not responding. Cast doubt into the minds of people, upset their ways of working and thinking, and they will, after a period of despair, begin to think afresh.

Sometimes, agents of change find the culture ready and willing: in the Exeter mental psychiatric services it had to be generated. But the 'Community' party gained confidence, and became convinced that if we did not choose to make the change, the Department of Health would one day foist it upon us. Better to take charge of our own destiny than be pawns in a centrally imposed game. By all these means, it became a matter, not of should the changes be made, but how soon. It is difficult to say how long this process of generating acceptance took, but two years seems a reasonable estimate.

### COMMITMENT TO CHANGE 'AT THE TOP' OF THE ORGANISATION IS VITAL

The interests, ambitions, energy and skill of the chief manager at the top of an organisation are significant factors in what happens to an organisation. That is accepted in public organisations today, but in 1974, when I first arrived in Exeter, the influence of individuals was not a fashionable concept and there was consensus management by teams of six people to keep it in check. It made the task of change harder, but not impossible.

At the time the mental hospitals reminded me of a nature film I once saw with a column of termites moving through the countryside and consuming everything in its path. A few white ants were sprinkled at the head of the column and in seconds the army was routed and scattered to the four winds. It struck me that we needed some white ants to disrupt the implacable march of the mental hospitals—all I had authority to do at that time was to appoint some as administrators and to work with them to show what was wanted.

## MANAGERS FOR CHANGE
## MUST BE CAREFULLY SELECTED

It was very important for the managers to be involved at every step and not at arms length. That included me, the chief administrator of the District—involvement could not be delegated. We all had to work in the crucible of change. It was an enterprise in which the individual's commitment and motives had to be clearly understood and trusted by everyone.

In those days each profession recruited its own staff. I had no say in the appointment of nursing officers and other staff brought into the hospitals, but I could change the type of administrators working there. So I recruited some bright young people to work with and support those professional staff within the system who wished to change it. But a job in a mental hospital was considered to blight a promising administrative career. Consequently, I adopted a solution introduced by the medical profession to fill junior posts in unpopular specialities: rotational appointments, which require the holders to work for periods in both popular and unpopular specialities. Many colleagues told me that the idea was impractical, but we did find people who were attracted by the scheme requiring them to work in mental hospitals as well as general hospitals. The best of them soon realised that there was real work to be done in the mental hospitals, and some stayed on to see the project through.

It is easy to see why politicians intent on radical reform find the public services so maddening. The officials are like a state orchestra with a set repertoire and every musician with a guaranteed place for life. They choose whether or not to respond to a new conductor, and are very unwilling to perform new works. Change requires people of commitment. One method of obtaining results from managers is to link performance to bonuses and short-term contracts. That is one way. But the changes in Exeter were accomplished with all the constraints of the old public service fully operational. It hardly mattered, for the staff you require are attracted by the management atmosphere they sense. Change was in the air, and the people interested in making it happen declared their interest. Those who found it unpalatable, left Exeter.

Later in the early 1980s the managers appointed were all recruited from within the staff of the District, and we were fortunate that so much ability had gathered over the years. They became committed to change for the same reasons as the professional staff and were not driven by external management mechanisms. Their motives could be trusted.

Shortly after the Exeter Health Authority was founded in 1981, the time was ripe to initiate the changes in mental health and mental handicap. There were four major projects and because team management was still in being, we required for each, a doctor, nurse and administrator. It was clear to me that while all the participating managers were needed, success in each project depended on the abilities of one of them, there had to be a leader. Teams were formed after much thought from staff already working in the District who shared an enthusiasm for the policies and ideas which had, by then, only been roughly sketched. They were all people who could accept responsibility for the broad but clear tasks they were given, and who were capable of working boldly and independently. They shared the attitude at the top, namely, that change would only happen if we make it happen. Their track records were known and they were usually people still capable of personal development. One very important feature was their shared human concern for the interests of all the hospital residents who would be affected. Also, they possessed the confidence to work in harmony with their staff and, in particular, the trade unions. Confidence and trust are infectious, and the most important ingredients in successful human endeavour.

To the silent majority the appointment of some new teams of managers was nothing new nor very threatening. There had been enthusiasts before. They had set out to do much and achieved little. The asylums stood impassive and daunting as unscaled mountains, apparently unaffected by mere human aspirations. To hearten the reformers, we had to find a way to convince the world we meant business.

### THE SIGNAL FOR CHANGE: A TIME-TABLE DECLARED FOR HOSPITAL CLOSURE

The management of change is action, not words.

Publishing a time-table for hospital closures was the method chosen to declare the change season open, and it concentrated everyone's attention. Simply announcing that the hospitals would close was not enough—it was essential to give a clear 'close by' date for each of them, not so far in the future that it could be put to the back of the mind, but one by which we could realistically anticipate that the job would be done. For every hospital we showed a simple diagram with a number of columns representing the period of years it was intended that the programme would take, usually three or four. At the bottom of every column was a reducing pile of boxes, representing ward closures, and above them an increasing number of community projects. Though the device was very simple, it became the main indicator for measuring that the programme was on the move and on target.

Constructing a building has the benefit of visualisation. First there are the drawings and then, as it rises out of the ground, tangible evidence of progress. A process of decentralisation lacks this opportunity for the eye to register the changes, but the simple diagrams gave the projects recognisable shape and clarity. The diagrams were included in the plans distributed for public consultation, were on display in the hospitals to keep staff informed, and pinned on the walls of manager's offices as a constant spur to action. We did not have to revise our initial timetables.

The moment of truth was moving from theory to action. Starcross was the first of our hospitals in which the management team was ready to swing into action. In October 1983 a plan was drafted for public consultation which proposed the setting up of local mental handicap services and the closure of Starcross Hospital by June 1986.

Once that decision was made the management teams at Exminster and Digby Hospitals were keen also to name a day. But here was a moment for careful timing. To have announced wholesale closure could have sparked a counter blast of public protest sufficient to halt any progress. Consequently, the individual closures were announced one by one over a period of some months and the feared public protests did not materialise.

The closure of the hospitals was visible for all to see, but the build up of local services less apparent. So it was necessary to show that residents and staff would have an assured future and that hospital assets were being recycled into new services which were indeed being opened before the hospitals closed. Getting right the timing of decisions was important throughout the programme, and that is a matter of judgement.

*INCENTIVES FOR CHANGE:*
*THE SAME MANAGERS CLOSE THE OLD*
*AND OPEN THE NEW, AND RELEASE*
*FUNDS ARE RING FENCED*

There is no more important feature of the management structure than to ensure that the managers developing the new community services are also responsible for closing the hospitals. To divide these responsibilities is a recipe for inactivity. If the task is simply to close a hospital, with no future planned for the staff or managers, there is a strong incentive to go slow. Likewise, community managers with little or no service to manage until somebody else closes a hospital, can easily become attached to a life filled with endless planning meetings and free from the hassles of operational management. This is not a theoretical point but one based on the observation of a number of projects. It is possibly one of the most important reasons why so many programmes of change make so little progress.

The key incentive driving the management teams in Exeter to close the hospitals was the knowledge that it was the only way for them to get the money to move on to the exciting work of setting up brand new services. Modernising services and moving them to a more appropriate setting by closing the old is positive and engenders enthusiasm.

Starcross would pay for the new mental handicap service for the Exeter District. Exminster's resources would provide the new mental health service in the Torbay and North Devon Districts and Digby would fund Exeter's mental health service.

The next crucial incentive was the knowledge that the psychiatric resources released would not be diverted for other purposes: the Health Authority had agreed that they would be protected or 'ring fenced'. In addition to these funds a decentralisation reserve, or bridging fund, had been created by the Authority from within its own resources, so that the programme had some working capital to get started. The nature of this fund is explained in Chapter 9.

The staff could see that their managers had the authority and the money to deliver the goods.

## CONFIDENCE FOR CHANGE COMES FROM DELEGATION AND TRUST

We wanted the managers and staff to be on the same side, working together to solve common problems and always with the hospital residents' interest uppermost. If staff and managers were at odds, the whole programme would be at risk.

Top managers had been given broad responsibilities and for so complex a programme to succeed it was important that they too should develop resourcefulness and responsibility in their subordinates. To do this it was necessary to delegate responsibilities for individual local projects to their managers. The culture of trusting people to get the job done had to permeate the whole organisation. It is no good pretending that there has been delegation if every decision has to be referred to another level for approval and errors are pounced upon. Being in the 'risk business' means accepting there will be some failures. Managers and their staff thrived in this atmosphere and, in fact, the failures were few.

The foundation of staff confidence was an agreement drawn up by the Trade Unions and the Exeter Health Authority in 1985, which guaranteed there would be no 'compulsory redundancy' resulting from the changes, but a job for all those who wanted to work in the new services. The agreement offered existing staff preferential consideration for any suitable vacancy on the Health Authority's payroll, and assistance to ease the transition. This agreement, District Procedure 17—universally known as DP17—has been one of the more controversial aspects of our programme of change. Some critics see it as a sign of management weakness, 'giving in to the trade unions, instead of dictating to them'. Others are critical that retaining former hospital staff would perpetuate the old institutional ways. There were also concerns that with no spur to find another job, many staff would sit tight and defend their right to no compulsory redundancy. Some of these criticisms are doubtless true, but DP17 got things going and enabled the changes to happen. Having to negotiate everything with trade unions added to the complexity of the management job and took a little longer, but the outcomes were effective and it did not delay any of the time targets set for opening the new services and closing the old.

Careful negotiation resulted in swift change. Most of the service innovations have been created and introduced by former hospital staff. Many of the foremost defenders of the old order became the keenest enthusiasts for the new style. It would have been totally inconsistent to believe that the patients could alter their ways but not the staff. There is no general evidence that Exeter's hospital staff were too institutionalised to adapt. In one sense staff have not changed because they always wanted the best for their patients. Although willing, some have found the changes difficult, and still today much effort goes into staff support and training.

The transfer of staff from the old hospitals to new job opportunities has uncannily kept in step. The reason for this is not difficult to explain. Management and trade unions realised that DP17 was an act of good faith and that if staff tried to hang on to their old jobs, despite hospital closure, the agreement would not have lasted for a day, and the Authority would have had to introduce compulsory redundancy. The goodwill of DP17 would have been destroyed, to the delight of our critics elsewhere in the system who were anxious to teach trade unions a lesson. That may sound far fetched, but it was indeed a real feature of management attitudes at the time. In consequence, the trade unions had as big an interest in ensuring DP17's effectiveness as did management. The staff have transferred during the four years when the big hospitals were closing, and there has been no attempt to frustrate the move by people clinging to the negative aspects of a 'no compulsory redunancy' agreement. Freed from anxieties about continuing em-

ployment, staff have been able to give their full attention to getting the new services right.

From time to time we had opportunities to show staff
that management's supportive attitude had not
changed. One occurred in 1985 when the Department of
Health required that Health Authorities must, according to a strict time-table, submit all their cleaning,
catering and laundry services to competitive tender on
the open market. This caused much trade union opposition nationally as well as in Exeter. It would require
considerable management effort, which would distract
us from our main task of recycling the mental hospitals.
But more serious still, it would mean that for many staff
DP17 would not be applicable, for if a commercial
contractor was successful we could not guarantee our
staff continued employment with the Authority.

Because we were in the middle of so many complex
changes, the Health Department's announcement of
this initiative could not have come at a worse time. It
could have driven our trade unions, who had risked so
much, to withdraw their co-operation with the closure
programme, and this in turn would have encouraged
many other opponents who were eager at the time to
see it slow down and stop. Exeter found good support
for its case to be treated differently at the Regional
Health Authority and among officials at Department of
Health, but the decision had to be taken by a Minister.
The problem was that there were many Health Authorities looking for the line to be broken and a precedent set
so that they too could argue for delay. Fortunately, it
was decided by a Minister that Exeter should be given
respite for eighteen months—sufficient time for the
closures to be effected. Our programme stayed on the
rails. This renewed confidence among staff that management was indeed on their side. The new time-table
for competitive tendering was subsequently completed
on time and with trade union support and co-operation.

Staff consultation, open management, and good access to information for staff, characterised the style
managers were required to adopt as they transformed

the services. For the hospital staff at Exminster and Digby, there were regular meetings where managers reported new information and answered questions. At the beginning only the hospital ballrooms could accommodate the large numbers of people attending. As the wards closed and staff numbers dwindled, the meetings took place in smaller rooms. One of the last to be held at Exminster was attended by no more than 50 people, the tail of an army which had once numbered 800. When asked what they now felt about the changes, one of those present summed it up for the others:

> 'At first I thought the hospital wouldn't close. But now I see the exciting things being done by staff who used to work here. The chance to get out and join them can't come soon enough for me.'

Open meetings are not enough on their own, for they cannot deal with individual worries. These need to be handled in personal interviews. Information is seldom benign, for it often triggers fresh worries. There is a need to have both kinds of meeting, and to be aware that neither will solve all anxieties. Provided that managers are aware of these consequences, I believe open management is still the best style for successful change.

### CONTROLLING CHANGE:
### STICKING TO THE TIME-TABLE AND
### STAYING WITHIN BUDGET

The time-table for change was set by the pace at which managers judged they could close the hospitals and thereby release resources. The Health Authority was keen to move fast and maintain momentum, and insisted on detailed six monthly progress reports throughout the years of change, to ensure that the milestones were passed on schedule. We resisted the idea of attempting to speed up closure—we did not want a race for some mythical blue riband awarded to the first to close. But none of the hospitals closed later than had originally been estimated. Joint meetings with union representatives at district and unit levels ensured that potential delays were averted, and hindrances removed.

Controlling the money was a work of both science and art. It is to the credit of the Treasurer, his colleages in the other Districts, and our managers that their constant struggles to keep within the fund available were achieved 'below stairs' and never became a problem for the Health Authority or the District Management Team.

There is a danger of making the whole process sound too easy. Fortunately, an atmosphere was engendered in which the majority of staff and managers, at all levels, have sought to make things work. As in all large projects, not everything has gone according to plan, and if staff had so chosen there were many occasions when shortcomings could have been used to embarrass the management. But instead of calling the press, or summoning the trade union, staff have rolled up their sleeves and solved problems.

One major benefit has been the continuity of key personalities. The same managers, professional leaders, trade union representatives, and Health Authority Members were around for the ten years of change. It is difficult to envisage how major change could occur without this continuity of key leaders.

## PATTERN MAKING:
### DESIGNING THE NEW SERVICES
### FROM SCRATCH

Closing hospitals was a very clear goal: but determining what would replace them was a matter almost without precedent. We had to find our own patterns to follow, and for this we had to rely on the imagination and ingenuity of the staff we were releasing from the hospitals. It was like taking an army trained in conventional manoeuvres and converting it into a guerrilla force. In the former the requirement was to follow established routines and orders. Now the army would be divided into small units whose success depended on the skill of local commanders.

Little advance training was possible—only after the new units were established and working could training needs begin to be understood. Training in the hospital atmosphere could defeat the purpose and inhibit the transition. Nobody had much idea of what challenges the community held, and I feared that too great an emphasis on training would be like trying to teach swimming in a classroom—the staff might never be ready to try the water. We moved the trainers out with a staff, so they could assist each other in real and not theoretical conditions. Usually it was possible for staff to gain some experience during the quieter times of an extended commissioning period, as new services worked up to their full operational levels.

To conventional planners the working methods in changes of this kind are unsatisfactory. The process is dynamic and not the usually accepted method of drawing up a comprehensive and detailed blueprint in advance of change. Everything has to be worked out as the project progresses, and experience gained from trial and error.

The first local support unit in the learning disability service was to have been the pattern for several more. But in practice it seemed too much like a small hospital and the style was not repeated. Another example of learning from experience was in the service for elderly people. There are now ten units for elderly confused people (HECs) used mainly as flexible resource centres providing support at home. Their inpatient accommodation is not intensively used—seldom for long stays, most often for respite care, crisis management, and re-assessment. Although the focus is not as orginally foreseen—staff, relatives, and private nursing homes have adapted to make good use of HEC resources for virtually all the confused elderly people in the locality.

The key element guiding our service planning has been to respond to the needs of the people for whom they are intended. This means consulting with them and their families, the better to understand their problems in coping with disabilities which cannot be 'cured', and providing for them where they live, or as close to home as possible. The responsibilities of the management teams for each of the new services included determining the style and philosophy of what was to be done, formulating the new patterns of delivery, training and preparing staff, and effecting the changes. It was a tall order for anyone taking on such responsibilities, and a particular management style was essential for the work to proceed. It was necessary to create an atmosphere in which people found encouragement, support, and assistance from the Health Authority and its managers. The emphasis had to be complimenting success rather than finding fault when things went wrong, as they often did. Only in this way could the managers and professional leaders work with confidence.

### MAINTAINING THE FLOW OF CHANGE: SYSTEMS BUILT IN TO KEEP THE NEW SERVICES RELEVANT TO CHANGING NEEDS

It could be easy to fall into the trap of thinking that the process of change is complete now that the community services are working and the principal hospitals have closed. But change will be ongoing. We were aware that our initial concepts of community services would be perhaps too influenced by our hospital experience. Just like the first car designers, we could create a 'horse-less carriage', something still under the strong influence of the recent past.

In any case, the momentum for change has been so hard won that nobody wants to see it stop.

Various measures have been built into the programmes to keep it rolling forward. There is an underlying requirement to involve and engage the users, so that by their contribution the services are responding to their needs. There is an effective Evaluation Team whose activities are constantly aimed at reshaping the work of local services, to make them relevant to the changing needs of their customers, both the former hospital residents and the new clientele. The service providers find these evaluations both helpful and reassuring.

One reason that the mental hospitals experienced a period of public criticism is that in their isolation they had not been exposed to changing attitudes and invigorating currents of criticism. There is no feeling in the new Exeter services that there has been too much change, and there is no desire to be shielded from public and professional comment.

Of all the things the staff have achieved, I believe this is the most important. For if they can stay alert to criticism and respond constructively to it, they will continue to grow and improve the services they offer. The changes and events of the last ten years do not mark the end of a task. They have been a preparation and training course for the future.

### TIMING AND ORCHESTRATION

Cause and effect follow one another only if they are brought into relationship. A kettle of water will boil only if it is put on the flame. The whole story I have told, of community services growing out of hospital closures, and a complex web of decisions and actions made to bring it about—cause and effect—happened only because it seemed inevitable. By now the reader will see that this 'inevitability' had to be constructed. A scenario had to be fashioned to convince all the actors in the piece that nothing else was possible. That is the role and skills of the producers, a task of imagination, of constantly turning events to advantage. Whether it is politics or management is for the theorists to decide. The simple fact is that it has to be done by somebody, or else the kettle goes off the boil.

### THE WILL FOR CHANGE:
### THE MOST IMPORTANT ELEMENT

The complexity and potential hazards of what we attempted are, in retrospect, daunting. If we had thought about them all carefully, there could have been argument for never starting. It is little wonder that so many such endeavours sink in a downward spiral at the planning stage, which 'proves' the whole strategy far too difficult to attempt. An act of faith is necessary, and the determination that eventually the enterprise will succeed.

The will to make things happen is the most important element in the whole business of managing change. The determination to make things happen, come what may, is something which leadership must contribute at all levels, from the top down, to inspire an intelligent doggedness and persistence throughout the organisation. It is not the only ingredient, but like garlic in a casserole it suffuses the whole dish. Nothing of significance will happen without it.

# 9

# Financial aspects:
# ways and means

## OVERVIEW

Lack of money is the excuse commonly given by health
authorities and social service departments for slow
progress with programmes for care in the community.
The Exeter experience indicates, however, that with
careful management there was already sufficient money
in the system to fund the change.

Confidence was given by protecting, 'ring fencing',
the psychiatric budgets so that money could not be
spirited away to other specialties when the mental
hospitals closed. An overdraft facility was set up by the
Health Authority, employing its own funds, and managers could use it to get the new community services
running before the old ones closed. Full use was also
made of Joint Finance opportunities (government mon-
ies given to all health and local authorities to encourage
community projects) and the discharged patients' individual entitlements to Social Security benefits.

We were not required to reduce overall expenditure
on mental health and mental handicap services, and
better value has been obtained from the new uses of the
capital and revenue previously invested in the hospitals. The opportunity has prompted imaginative ways to
promote business activity to the financial benefit and
advantage of the clients of the services.

## CAN WE AFFORD CARE IN THE
## COMMUNITY?
## A PRECEDENT HAD CAST DOUBT

In the early 1970s the Department of Health had funded
a community mental health project, known as the Wor-

cester Experiment. It was reputed to have cost at least an extra £·5m annually beyond what the health authority was already spending on mental health services. What is more, the old mental hospital, Powick, which many thought the new services were designed to replace, had not closed. Somehow the notion grew that a Health Authority planning reform would need at least a £·5m extra revenue per annum to convert from hospital to community services. Some advocates for reform argued that no change should commence until the Health Department found the additional money.

This strategy did not commend itself to us, and we decided to get on despite what some regarded as a shortage of essential funds. Indeed, when we embarked on the changes in Exeter there was no proof that the exercise would be financially viable. We simply had a hunch that it could be done within the funds available. Fortunately, nobody asked for a costed programme, for we could not have provided it. We did however establish a number of principles for the programme's financial policy.

## PRINCIPLES OF FINANCIAL POLICY

### RING FENCING THE PSYCHIATRIC BUDGETS

First we needed a method to ensure that not a penny less of revenue would be spent on psychiatric services in the community than had been spent in the mental hospitals. The motives for hospital closure were regarded by many with great suspicion. People feared that in the process of closing mental hospitals the released money might be subtly palmed into other pockets, particularly into general hospital services which have an enormous potential for development and thereby an insatiable appetite for extra resources. Ring fencing reassured the staff of the psychiatric services without exciting the concerns of staff in the general hospitals who feared that there would be major investment of new money into the psychiatric services. It has been a potent factor in maintaining the support of all interest groups that there has been no leakage of psychiatric funds to other services.

### FAIR SHARES FOR CLIENT DISTRICTS

A method had to be devised to give confidence to all the health districts the hospitals served. Royal Western Counties (mental handicap) and Exe Vale (mental illness) admitted patients from five health districts in Devon and Cornwall, including Exeter. It was essential in the decentralisation of services that these other districts would benefit from the funds released by the hospital closures so that they could establish their own local services. It was also important that the local government councils with their responsibilities for planning, housing and social services, should also be involved. Formulae were evolved by consultation to guarantee a fair division of the proceeds, so that each Health Authority could demonstrate clear development of new services, and not simply the closure of old hospitals.

Dividing up the hospital resources pro rata to the population of each district seems quite a simple and equitable matter, but the use made of the hospitals bore no relationship to district populations. The host district, Exeter, admitted far more local patients than those distant from the hospitals. There were also patients who had been in the hospitals for so long that they had no real home district. Their needs too had to be catered for, complicating neat financial apportionments.

The solution adopted for mental handicap services was to transfer sufficient resources to the Health Authority in each hospital resident's home district. Exeter Health Authority is paid by that Authority until the client moves back home, or elsewhere. Some long-term residents originating from other Devon districts have chosen to remain in Exeter, so that payment will continue for them for the remainder of their lives.

For mental health services the method was different. The funds were divided in relation to the relative size of district populations. In simple terms this meant that Exeter received a smaller share than the amount of hospital resources it had been using, whereas Torbay and North Devon gained. The debate has been endless, and it highlights the accidental way in which budgets for individual specialities accumulate historically and without any objective decisions about the amounts actually needed in each location. Priorities in health are constantly argued, but there is no sensible way for deciding what should be spent, for example, an ophthalmology compared with dermatology.

Nevertheless, the various Health Authorities were able to sort out among themselves arrangements for the division of the hospital resources. An equitable division has now largely been accomplished to the satisfaction of the participants. The Exeter Health Authority has been the broker in these matters, and an essential feature of this role has been to avoid giving any impression that advantage was being made to gain for itself the lion's share of resources. Any other Health Authority attempting a similar course is well advised to bear this lesson in mind: that as the initiator, Exeter chose to exercise a degree of magnanimity to sustain the confidence of all parties. At no time has it been necessary to call in external referees.

Table 4 shows how the funds have been redistributed

TABLE 4 *Re-allocation of mental health revenue resources (amounts adjusted for inflation to 1986 value)*

| HEALTH DISTRICTS | ORIGINAL USAGE (MENTAL HOSPITALS) | FINAL USAGE (COMMUNITY CARE) | |
|---|---|---|---|
| | m | m | |
| EXETER | 8·0 | 5·5 | −31% |
| TORBAY | 2·6 | 4·6 | +77% |
| NORTH DEVON | 1·3 | 1·8 | +38% |
| | 11·9 | 11·9 | |

from Exeter to the other health districts. Perhaps the most fascinating thing is that the most exciting period in the development of Exeter's mental health services since the 1840s was carried out at a time when its use of resources was apparently being reduced by a self inflicted 30% cut.

### BRIDGING FINANCE: LOCALLY FUNDED OVERDRAFT FACILITIES

Funds were needed in Exeter to make possible the management requirement that new services should open before the old ones closed. The financial mechanism for a health service is no different from that of any individual who buys a new house before selling the old: bridging funds or overdraft facilities are needed.

The only possible source of any large sums of money was the Exeter Health Authority's own capital and revenue allocations. The solution presented itself from the answer to another problem facing the Health Authority—and applying some lateral thinking. In the early 1980s there were plans to build and commission a new suite of orthopaedic theatres and some additional geriatric wards in Exeter's central acute hospitals. The NHS at the time abounded with examples of capital projects being built and left empty for lack of revenue funds to employ staff and provide other essential running costs. We were fortunate in enjoying a small growth each year of revenue funds—increments which increased the total regular income thereafter. The estimates for the annual running costs of the two projects would consume the total of two years' growth, leaving no money for any other projects. Two years of famine for all other medical specialties would be a privation hardly likely to pass without controversy, so the Treasurer and I decided to save up a small sum every year in advance so that by the time the buildings were ready there would be a reserve of revenue funds for them.

The problem was how to protect this revenue reserve from other possible uses. The lateral thinking was to employ it as the bridging fund for the psychiatric

patients of mental hospitals have established for those in similar need to themselves. Not only are they often more in tune with the needs of the people they cater for, but they also make better use of money. There are many people with the wit and ability to work in a professional capacity, but because of their disability (either physical or mental) employers are unwilling to offer them jobs. Consequently, they dedicate their efforts to the service of fellow sufferers, whose plight they well understand. Better use of money comes from not paying themselves either the rates or conditions which are demanded by professional staff. For example, professionally provided services are often closed at the weekends because of higher running costs, penal rates of pay, and the desire of staff to have their weekends free. Better services arise from their understanding and sympathy with the needs of people like themselves—they are both consumers and providers.

These consumer-provided services score on two counts: they more frequently understand and respond to their customers' needs, and they empower those who organise them so that they truly become independent.

## 3. THE NEED TO CHALLENGE PROFESSIONAL COMPLACENCY

Professional training is excellent at teaching intelligent people what to do. It is far too efficient at training them not to think about why they are doing it.

The whole process which led to the closure of the institutions started by having the gall to ask what was happening in the hospitals—what work was being done, why, and whether there might not be better ways. So aloof have been the caring professions that anyone posing such simple questions has been seen off with imperious glares. Restrictive and unquestioning work practices are as much a problem for the middle as the working classes. Work study or operational research is needed to oblige professionals to examine what they are doing and whether it is in the best interests of their clients.

The questions should be: what human needs are we trying to serve? What can we do to meet these needs? What are we actually doing and is it relevant?

Once we had exposed the inadequacies of the old system by this kind of questioning, we found no shortage of staff volunteers to help set up better alternatives. The experience demonstrated to me that those oft vilified armies of public service staff can be as flexible and cooperative as the much vaunted Japanese workers. In both instances it seems to be because they were given a clear vision of an improving future by management, the chance to employ their ingenuity in achieving it, and an underlying security of employment. Wooden attitudes from staff are only a response to wooden approaches by management, and if there is not a meeting of minds and agreement on purposes the battle will continue with sometimes one side seeming to win and sometimes the other. Solid and inflexible trade union attitudes have been a feature of large and unyielding institutions. But it was by these trade unions and their numbers that the changes were made—probably because we treated each other like fellow human beings, and built up mutual confidence and trust. It really has been a silly feature of the 1960s and 1970s that people seem to have been influenced by caricatured portrayals of management and trade union attitudes instead of getting to know the people they are working with, discovering common concerns, and doing something about them.

## 4. LESSONS FOR OTHER HEALTH SERVICES

A distinction is sometimes drawn in health services between those concerned with 'care'—looking after people whose condition cannot be transformed by medical intervention, and those whose business is to 'cure'—restoring an impaired function by medical or surgical action. This book is about the former category and for a long time I assumed that 'caring' services were, somehow, second rate medical services in the sense that they lack the scientific rigour associated with 'curing' services. With this in mind, it seemed to me that the changes we found to be necessary in the mental health and mental handicap services, however fascinating, were of no relevance to main stream medical services and their management.

How mistaken I was, for all the lessons learned from the examination and change experience of the psychiatric services apply equally to all other medical services. It is just that it takes more stamina to challenge surgeons or physicians, for they tend to be so certain of the rightness of what they do. Sadly, I have heard clinical freedom used as an excuse to avoid having to justify the status quo rather than explore alternatives. Requiring patients to stay in hospital for a night or two for procedures which can be performed on a day basis is both an inconvenience to patients and waste of health funds as keeping people in a psychiatric hospital who could live in the community. Grouping on a general hospital campus services which should be more dispersed and informally provided is as inappropriate as any of the examples given in the preceding pages.

Far from being an irrelevant excursion, the experience of change in the 'care' services described in this book provides information to assist the analysis of all health services.

## CONCLUSION: WHY PSYCHIATRIC SERVICES IN OTHER PARTS OF THE COUNTRY HAVE NOT YET CHANGED

There are no two ways about it, when all these changes were occurring, we were very keen to be the first past the post. I can still recall the shock of discovering in 1981, from a newspaper report, that the Italians had apparently beaten us hands down. A law had been enacted which required the closure of their mental hospitals, and all in a day. We later discovered that only one hospital closed, in Trieste, and the report had been too optimistic—or pessimistic, depending on your point of view.

From all the interest shown, and all the plans we learned about, it appeared that we might be leading, but only by a short head. Once more we were mistaken. Psychiatry has never attracted much managerial attention and this still seems to be the case. Firstly, it is by no means accepted that converting mental hospitals to community services is the right thing to do. Secondly, even where there seems to be support for the idea, the energy, or some spark, is lacking to actually get on with the job.

The same doubts and concerns are raised now in other places, that were raised and answered in Exeter, five and more years ago. I am aware of regions where the problem is not lack of money for bridging funds —they exist but are not called upon. I can only assume that the task is regarded as being just too hard to attempt.

It is quite certain that the mental hospitals will not close themselves and that the inappropriate services they offer and the money they waste will continue, until there is resolute management action to convert it all into better health value for money. The conclusions I have come to are that at best it will take a great deal longer than I had thought, and at worst, that the hospitals will continue indefinitely.

The results in Exeter stand with a growing handful of other examples to show that people with the spirit to make necessary changes can indeed learn from the experiences of others, and improve on them, for the benefit of all.

Still they stand in Exeter, isolated, majestic and daunting out of the countryside—the asylums which our forefathers built with such solidity. The buildings are there—or at any rate, some of them—but they are no longer mental hospitals. They and the services they

once housed have been recycled. Mental health and
handicap services in Exeter have moved on from the
mental hospitals

# Exeter Health Authority

## *Reports of the Evaluation and Service Development Team*

1. *'I Can't Walk on the Moors Any More...'*
–developing services for older people to match local need in Okehampton locality and district.

2. *'Tell them 'thank you very much'*
–community support for dementia sufferers and their families in Exmouth.

3. *'Mental Health Matters'*
–evaluation of the Tiverton community mental health team Leigh House, Tiverton.

4. *'When people think you are mad they start behaving in very odd ways.'*
–developing services for people with severe long term mental health problems in Exeter City.

5. *'Working Together... For Older People in Crediton Locality'*

6. *'Views of Budleigh...'*
–improving services for older people in Budleigh Salterton.

7. *'First Footings'*
–the first years of a local service for people suffering from dementia in Tiverton/Cullompton.

*Getting closer to the consumer? Locality planning in the Exeter Health District* by TONY DAY. Available from Publications Department, School for Advanced Urban Studies, Rodney Lodge, Grange Road, Bristol BS8 4EA.

# Exeter Health Authority

## *Mental Handicap and Mental Health services by localities in the Exeter District*

### CREDITON LOCALITY (Pop. 18,000)

1. COMMUNITY MENTAL HANDICAP TEAM     CREDITON

2. COMMUNITY HOME     'Brooklyn',
   5 places Mental handicap adults     CREDITON

3. COMMUNITY HOME     'Copple Court',
   6 places Mental handicap adults     CREDITON

4. COMMUNITY HOME     'Cromwells',
   3 places Mental handicap adults     CREDITON

5. COMMUNITY HOME     'Highbank',
   3 places Mental handicap adults     CREDITON

6. COMMUNITY HOME     'Olcote',
   3 places Mental handicap adults     CREDITON

7. COMMUNITY HOME     'Sepia',
   3 places Mental handicap adults     CREDITON

8. LOCAL SUPPORT UNIT     'Dean View',
   6 places Mental handicap adults     CREDITON

9. COMMUNITY MENTAL HEALTH TEAM     CREDITON

10. HOME FOR THE ELDERLY                    'Boniface',
    CONFUSED                                CREDITON
       20 beds Assessment, rehabilitation
       and day care and community support


# EXMOUTH/BUDLEIGH SALTERTON LOCALITIES
## (Pop. 42,000)

1. COMMUNITY MENTAL HANDICAP          Stoke Lyne House,
   TEAM                               EXMOUTH

2. COMMUNITY HOME                            'Cedars',
      6 places Mental handicap adults        EXMOUTH

3. COMMUNITY HOME                             'Elms',
      6 places Mental handicap adults        EXMOUTH

4. COMMUNITY HOME                   'Gardeners Cottage',
      3 places Mental handicap      BUDLEIGH SALTERTON
      adults

5. LOCAL SUPPORT UNIT                       'Ellerslu',
      6 places Mental handicap adults       EXMOUTH

6. LOCAL SUPPORT UNIT                       'The Lodge',
      3 places Mental handicap adults        EXMOUTH

7. DAY CENTRE                         OUTMOOR CENTRE,
      Mental handicap adults               EXMOUTH

8. COMMUNITY MENTAL HEALTH TEAM               EXMOUTH

9. HOME FOR THE ELDERLY               'ST JOHN'S COURT',
   CONFUSED                               EXMOUTH
      20 beds Assessment,
      rehabilitation and day care
      and community support

## TIVERTON/CULLOMPTON LOCALITIES
### (Pop. 45,000)

1. COMMUNITY MENTAL HANDICAP TEAM — TIVERTON

2. COMMUNITY HOME
   6 places Mental handicap adults — 'Pine Lodge', TIVERTON

3. COMMUNITY HOME
   6 places Mental handicap adults — 'Bryher', TIVERTON

4. COMMUNITY HOME
   3 places Mental handicap children — 11 Barnes Close, CULLOMPTON

5. HOSTEL AND LOCAL SUPPORT UNIT
   11 places Mental handicap adults — 'Esther Mollard House', TIVERTON

6. LOCAL SUPPORT UNIT
   6 places Mental handicap adults — 'Greenways', TIVERTON

7. COMMUNITY MENTAL HEALTH TEAM — TIVERTON

8. HOME FOR THE ELDERLY CONFUSED
   20 beds Assessment, rehabilitation and day care and community support — 'Melrose', TIVERTON

## HONITON/AXMINSTER/SEATON/SIDMOUTH/ OTTERY ST MARY LOCALITIES (Pop. 61,000)

1. COMMUNITY MENTAL HANDICAP TEAM — HONITON

2. COMMUNITY HOME
   6 places Mental handicap adults — 5 & 6 Morton Way, AXMINSTER

3. COMMUNITY HOME                     'Greenacres',
   4 places Mental handicap adults            AXMINSTER

4. COMMUNITY HOME                 33 Monkton Road,
   6 places Mental handicap adults            HONITON

5. COMMUNITY HOME             11 & 12 Lyme Close,
   5 places Mental handicap adults            AXMINSTER

6. COMMUNITY HOME               8 & 9 Gronau Close,
   6 places Mental handicap adults            HONITON

7. COMMUNITY HOME          78 & 80 Sandhill Street,
   6 places Mental handicap adults        OTTERY ST. MARY

8. COMMUNITY HOME             70 Woodbury Park,
   3 places Mental handicap adults            AXMINSTER

9. COMMUNITY HOME            140 Harepath Road,
   6 places Mental handicap adults             SEATON

10. COMMUNITY HOME               5 Seafield Road,
    10 places Mental handicap adults           SEATON

11. LOCAL SUPPORT UNIT                 'Hillcrest',
    6 places Mental handicap adults            HONITON

12. LOCAL SUPPORT UNIT                 'Lisburne',
    6 places Mental handicap adults            HONITON

13. COMMUNITY MENTAL HEALTH TEAM            HONITON

14. HOME FOR THE ELDERLY CONFUSED       'Kingfisher',
    9 beds Assessment, rehabilitation          SEATON
    and day care and community
    support

15. HOME FOR THE ELDERLY CONFUSED        'Conyleave',
    9 beds Assessment,                    AXMINSTER
    rehabilitation and day care
    and community support

16. HOME FOR THE ELDERLY CONFUSED         HONITON
    20 beds Assessment,
    rehabilitation and day care
    and community support

17. HOME FOR THE ELDERLY CONFUSED        'Sedemuda',
    20 beds Assessment,                   SIDMOUTH
    rehabilitation and day care
    and community support


## EXETER LOCALITIES (Pop. 118,000)

1. COMMUNITY MENTAL HANDICAP              EXETER
   TEAM

2. COMMUNITY HOME                        'Carnanton',
   8 places Mental handicap adults         EXETER

3. COMMUNITY HOME                     13/14 Coronation
   6 places Mental handicap adults          Terrace,
                                      STARCROSS, DEVON

4. COMMUNITY HOME                         'Glenlyn',
   6 places Mental handicap           EXMINSTER, DEVON
   adults

5. COMMUNITY HOME                      'Fern Cottage',
   4 places Mental handicap           EXMINSTER, DEVON
   adults

6. COMMUNITY HOME                     1 Hospital Lane,
   3 places Mental handicap adults        Whipton,
                                           EXETER

7. COMMUNITY HOME                     2 Hospital Lane,
   3 places Mental handicap adults        Whipton,
                                           EXETER

8.  COMMUNITY HOME                         Longcombe,
    5 places Mental handicap adults           EXETER

9.  COMMUNITY HOME                    'Lydford House',
    10 places Mental handicap adults          EXETER

10. COMMUNITY HOME                          1, 2 & 3
    3 places Mental handicap          Road Cottages,
    adults each                       DAWLISH EXETER

11. COMMUNITY HOME                          Fernley,
    9 places Mental handicap adults           EXETER

12. COMMUNITY HOME                         Budlake,
    5 places Mental handicap adults           EXETER

13. COMMUNITY HOME                 57, 59, 61 and 63
    12 places Mental handicap   Whipton Barton Road,
    adults                                    EXETER

14. COMMUNITY HOME                 1, 2, 3, 4 Windsor
    12 places Mental handicap          Drive, DAWLISH
    adults

15. COMMUNITY HOME                 'Wellpark House',
    8 places Mental handicap adults           EXETER

16. COMMUNITY HOME                         'Merthyr',
    6 places Mental handicap adults        EXMINSTER

17. HOSTEL                                    Flat 1,
    8 places Mental handicap       Franklyn House,
    adults                                    EXETER

18. LOCAL SUPPORT UNIT                        Flat 2,
    7 places Mental handicap       Franklyn House,
    adults                                    EXETER

19. LOCAL SUPPORT UNIT                        Flat 3,
    6 places Mental handicap       Franklyn House,
    adults                                    EXETER

20. LOCAL SUPPORT UNIT                  Knightshayes,
    7 places Mental handicap adults           EXETER

21. LOCAL SUPPORT UNIT                                          'Broadoak',
    5 places Mental handicap adults                              EXETER

22. COMMUNITY MENTAL HEALTH                                       EXETER
    TEAM

23. ACUTE UNIT                                           Wonford House
    70 beds Mental illness adults                            Hospital,
                                                              EXETER

24. ACUTE UNIT                                                 'Cedars',
    43 beds Mental illness adults                              EXETER

25. CHILD, ADOLESCENT AND FAMILY                                 EXETER
    COMMUNITY TEAMS

26. CHILD, ADOLESCENT AND FAMILY                              'Larkby',
    COMMUNITY UNIT   12 beds                                   EXETER

27. CHILD, ADOLESCENT AND FAMILY                            'Matford',
    COMMUNITY UNIT   6 beds                                    EXETER

28. REHABILITATION UNIT                                  Russell Clinic,
    18 beds Mental illness adults                             EXETER

29. COMMUNITY REHABILITATION TEAM                               EXETER

30. REHABILITATION HOSTEL                        Sannerville Chase,
    6 places Mental illness adults                            EXETER

31. REHABILITATION HOSTEL                            Belmont Home,
    6 places Mental illness adults                            EXETER

32. REHABILITATION HOSTEL                           Spurfield Home,
    12 places Mental illness adults                           EXETER

33. REHABILITATION HOSTEL                           Colleton Lodge,
    12 places Mental illness adults                           EXETER

34. REHABILITATION HOSTEL                       Warkworth House,
    12 places Mental illness adults                           EXETER

35. REHABILITATION WORK SKILLS UNIT              Bell Industries,
                                                             EXETER

36.  DAY CARE SUPPORT          (a)  Cavalier Club
                               (b)  Friendship Centre
                               (c)  Meadow House
                               (d)  Redhills House
                               (e)  Springboard Project,
                                            EXETER

37.  HOME FOR THE ELDERLY CONFUSED          'Leycombe'
     20 beds Assessment, rehabilitation       EXETER
     and day care and community support

38.  HOME FOR THE ELDERLY CONFUSED          'Franklyn',
     20 beds Assessment, rehabilitation       EXETER
     and day care and community support

## OKEHAMPTON LOCALITY (Pop. 17,000)

1.  COMMUNITY MENTAL HANDICAP TEAM          OKEHAMPTON

2.  COMMUNITY HOME                          'The Croft',
     3 places Mental handicap adults         OKEHAMPTON

3.  LOCAL SUPPORT UNIT                       'The Bartons',
     6 places Mental handicap adults         OKEHAMPTON

4.  COMMUNITY MENTAL HEALTH TEAM            OKEHAMPTON

5.  HOME FOR THE ELDERLY CONFUSED           'Redvers',
     9 beds Assessment, rehabilitation       OKEHAMPTON
     and day care and community support

DAVID KING

# Moving on from mental hospitals to community care

## A CASE STUDY OF CHANGE IN EXETER

DAVID KING

# Moving on from mental hospitals to community care

## A CASE STUDY OF CHANGE IN EXETER

The Nuffield Provincial
Hospitals Trust

Published by the
Nuffield Provincial Hospitals Trust
3 Prince Albert Road, London NW1 7SP
ISBN 0 900574 77 1
©Nuffield Provincial Hospitals Trust, 1991

Designed by Bernard Crossland
PRINTED IN GREAT BRITAIN BY
BURGESS & SON (ABINGDON) LTD
THAMES VIEW, ABINGDON
OXFORDSHIRE

Cover illustration by New Zealand
artist Mary Taylor

# FOREWORD

After the end of World War II, reformers of social and health policy in Britain, and in some other countries, became convinced that the confinement of mentally ill people in large institutions is both dehumanising and anti-therapeutic. At one level it robs the people kept there of freedom, privacy, and normal social contact; it also denies them responsibility and control of crucial aspects of their lives. At a time when people were increasingly demanding 'rights' rather than benevolence, there was obvious cause to challenge such a system. But there was another, equally valid, reason for demanding change, when successive studies in the 50s and 60s showed that prolonged and inappropriate hospitalisation was positively inimical to modern methods of psychiatric treatment.

Yet despite the inclusion of community care in the 1959 Mental Health Act as the most appropriate form of care for mentally ill people, action to provide it was desperately slow. Nearly thirty years passed before the government was publicly committed to the idea of a comprehensive, integrated, community care system, accessible to people with mental health problems wherever they happen to live. Without farsighted managers and practitioners who, like David King, were prepared to take risks and introduce community care in their own areas, without waiting for official endorsement, the concept would have been even slower to take hold. It was essential to show that it was possible to transfer services from hospital to community and—although the policy is based on better care, not saving of money—that it is financially feasible. The success of the pioneering community mental health care services established in Devon proved beyond doubt that they *could* be provided, and that the people who use them find them infinitely preferable to the large old institutions they replaced.

The trend towards providing care for mentally ill people in the community has not been a purely British phenomenon, but is part of a world wide movement. As Britain becomes more involved in Europe, it is interesting to recall the statement at the end of the Council of Europe's Second Conference of European Heath Ministers in 1985 'reaffirming the importance of mental health promotion and the prevention of disorders as essential components of a comprehensive policy .... area based and geared to the needs and active participation of those interested and of the public'.

The World Health Organisation and other international bodies have acknowledged that Britain has taken the lead in finding acceptable alternatives to mental hospital care. This book, describing the actual experience of moving away from an outdated institution-based system, to one more suited to the needs of the 21st century, offers inspiration as well as practical knowledge to the many places (in Britain as well as in other countries) where large mental hospitals continue to provide the main form of care.

EDITH MORGAN
*Founder President,*
*European Regional Council*
*World Federation for Mental Health.*

# CONTENTS

## APPENDICES

# INTRODUCTION

After more than a century of service the Victorian mental hospitals have reached the end of their useful lives. For many years the numbers of patients in them have slowly dwindled and in consequence, costs have risen but the same cannot be said for the standards of service. Plans to replace the mental hospitals by a new style of service characterised as 'community care' (a mix of local domiciliary, ambulatory and short stay hospital care), first mooted in the 60s, have failed to materialise because of lack of money and the conviction to see them come to pass. This lack of resolve stems in part from perceived problems in the alternative to the mental hospitals for community care, as it is currently envisaged, does not provide all the answers. Yet the mental hospitals have had their day and it is time for the world to move on and find, by trial and error, better styles of service paid for in large part by the resources now locked up in the hospitals.

This is an account of the work of many hundreds of people in one corner of England. So far as we know, they achieved a first in the U.K., or—come to that—anywhere in the world. Their achievement was to develop comprehensive community mental health and mental handicap services by using the resources released from the closure of old mental hospitals. They were motivated by one well intentioned and driving purpose: to make a reality of the concept that people with mental illness and mental handicap should no longer be excluded from ordinary life but share in it. Nineteenth century ideas had created institutions designed to separate such people from society. Devon had its full share of these institutions and now, thanks to the efforts of the people who once worked in them, the remote and isolated hospitals have been replaced by a set of comprehensive services designed to meet the needs of their clients, and based in the communities in which they live.

xiii

I was privileged to work with them in a position which called for imagination and leadership. But my job was no more important than any other, for we were all inter-dependent. Nobody was more important than another, for without every individual contribution it would not have happened.

The events to be related are an example of ordinary people deciding of their own accord to get on with things. At a time when ordinary people have decided to overturn massive empires, it may seem of comparatively slight importance. But it shows what can be done when people choose to take the matter of reform into their own hands.

I have written this as a tribute to all those who took part. Names have been excluded, for it would be impracticable to include them all. More difficult than that, would be to attempt an assessment of their individual contributions.

The experience was one of the happiest and most fulfilling times of my life, and I believe it was so for others too. The joy of it all was to work with so many people united in a single purpose. To each and every one of them I am grateful for the experience shared. That would be enough, but there was the added pleasure of the response from all those we helped to release from the hospitals. They have shown how wrong it was for them to have been there and how much they have appreciated their new lease on life.

The long time it has taken me to complete the task led me to think that Devon's contribution would be swept aside by other examples and stirring events, as 'care in the community', with its implication of recycling the mental hospitals, became a national movement of giant proportions. That has not been the case—more's the pity. So the story still needs to be told to encourage others.

The account is simply my view of what took place, why and how. Others who took part will have a different perspective. So big a medley of projects calls for other accounts and these will be as reliable as mine, for in history there is no one complete statement. I hope that at least one of these takes a more 'nuts and bolts' approach for those readers who will be disappointed that my broad brush does not include the detailed 'how to do it' instructions.

I am most grateful to Michael Ashley-Miller, of the Nuffield Provincial Hospital Trust, for his insistence that I should write it—and his patience in waiting for me to complete the task. Jeanette Crossley and Kate Smiley have put up with my delays and ordered the sentences and paragraphs so that it makes a coherent account. I thank them both.

Edith Morgan has been a constant source of support through the years of change and I am pleased she has chosen to write a foreword.

I hope that this account will give encouragement and ideas to anyone embarking on a similar task. I hope also that it will help those who are anxious about the disappearance of the mental hospitals to understand that the exercise was not to reduce or cheapen services, nor to cast people in need of care into an uncaring society—but to improve matters for them.

DAVID KING

*Auckland*                                    *February 1991*